The Possible Someone

The Possible Someone

The Possible Someone

THE POSSIBLE SOMEONE

The Possible Someone

THE POSSIBLE SOMEONE
(Complexity and Characterization for Advanced Actors)

David Scott

www.davidscott.ie

Selling a picture is like sending a blind child into a room full of razorblades. It's going to get hurt and it's never been hurt before. It doesn't know what hurt is.

John Logan, RED

The Possible Someone

In memory of Philip Seymour Hoffman

CONTENTS

The Possible Someone

FOREWORD

It's February 6 2014 and my third book is nearly finished, so I've taken some time to write this foreword today. Now will come the long process of poring over these pages and making sure it's exactly what I want to say, said in the most understandable language for my students. I find the odd hours to work on it during the day, as I am now, while my children are at school. In the evenings I head to my latest Company D Theatre production, Donald Margulies' "Collected Stories". It's up and open, so as director I have little to do other than be present. However I also like to give the front of house announcement. It's an unusual one this time because on February 2, last Sunday during our tech rehearsal, Philip Seymour Hoffman was found dead at the age of forty-six in his apartment in Manhattan. "Collected Stories" speaks of Delmore Schwartz, the mad poet of the fifties being found dead at a similarly premature age also in New York having destroyed himself on drink, smoke and Dexedrine. The resonances are too apparent to ignore, and so we dedicated the production to Philip's memory and I say as much in the announcement.

That's all very nice, as Ruth says in "Collected Stories", however I have found that the death of Philip has caused a kind of grief in me that is surprising. It's hurting much more than the death of a complete stranger should. I've tried to work it out in my mind, pushing it away as self-indulgent and perhaps pretentious, but it keeps coming back. So I've stopped trying to push it away and rather work out why I can't stop thinking about him. Perhaps it's the intimate relationship I had with his work, studying it and analyzing his choices. Perhaps it's the fact that I have written about Philip in this book and will have to go back, edit things and change "the kind of work Seymour Hoffman does" to "the kind of work Seymour Hoffman *did*". That will be sad, but it's more than that too.

Acting is changing. The personality actor is finally beginning to slip into antiquity. They were wonderful and they changed much and so the De Niros and Pacinos and their predecessors like Dean and Brando and Clift are now being moved from our contemporary psyches onto a shelf of honor to which we can refer. These changes, however, have meant a new evolutionary period in the art of acting. This evolution-revolution has been going on for around twenty years, albeit quietly, and it is led by five actors, three of whom are dead and a very small number of teachers.

In this new period of acting, the character has taken precedence over the personality of the actor probably for the first time in history, and certainly in the fullest way it ever has. For anyone who has trained with me in my studios, this is the ethic of the entire technique. The concept that the character has a unique essence, a life of its own, a complex personality that must be found by the actor, is driving a new way of acting that takes the ego of the actor him or herself, shoves it in a box and sticks it under the bed so that the work can be done. The focus of the work, the art of the work, is the selfless creation of a unique human being, and the telling of the story of that unique human being. Using theatre, characters and roles to promote oneself is a cringe-inducing practice now that was once considered both normal and necessary in this dog-eat-dog business. But I've never lived by that, and neither have my contemporaries. Acting is an art form that cannot be exploited. Theatre especially will turn around and bite you if you try to manipulate it as such. So we make our theatre and write our movies and we try to tell stories and tell them well for the art of it, not because we want fame and praise and cash, but because we're called to do it.

I remember Philip saying in an interview that he hoped only that he would be able to ride his bike to his off-off Broadway theatre jobs and that would be a happy career for him. The fact that he rose to the heights that he did in terms of fame was a complete surprise. In doing exactly that, he woke an American Industry to the potential for anyone to become a superstar if they can act. No one has done that since Dean and the "business" had forgotten it. The Industry seeks that which will make it money and so it immediately assumes pretty, booby girls and pretty, chiseled boys are the way to build fan-bases and make quick bucks. And they may be right, but Philip stood on the red carpet and waved his big hand at the cameras and said, "remember the actor? The actor who plays characters rather than himself? That's what we're trying to do here after all... isn't it?"

All my life I have been hunting my own white whale. That's not an easy thing to define. It's a way of acting that is pervasive, penetrating, artistic, absorbing and physical. It's not about this clumsy idea of "the obliteration of self". Self doesn't even come into it. There's no self to obliterate. It's not about debating these antiquated notions of "starting from the inside and working out, or starting from the outside and working in". It's not about keeping up this idea that there are physical actors and psychological actors and they're kind of on two opposing teams, Bogart verses Strasberg and so on. I've studied all this stuff for decades now. I've taught a lot of it and made it work for hundreds of actors in institutes and academies, but in my own studio my students pass through this brambly wood and we go out the other side and onto an ocean, searching for that white whale that surfaces at the end of the training and the work on the script. All this argument serves as a distraction and nothing more.

On that boat are many actors I've trained that you will not know. The establishment is not ready for them and could not possibly be able to understand the levels they are working on, although I live in hope that some day soon they will let them in. However in America and Australia we lost River Phoenix who had just glimpsed the whale, Heath Ledger who had seen the white and touched the beast's back, and now Philip Seymour Hoffman who had not only touched it, but seemed to have absorbed it into himself. The whiteness of the whale had enfolded him like a shroud. He acted with abandon and yet within the essence of the character. We were looking at a character that *was* the story itself, fully formed in every aspect and yet never did I feel like I was watching the mechanics of acting clunking away or an actor intruding on the story-telling with his own personality.

Still on that boat is Toni Collette and Daniel Day-Lewis, and it's those whose work I'll continue to study and there are a few others of course too, but not many in the public arena. Journalists cry out that Philip cannot be replaced. It's as if there are suddenly no more actors in the world. It's not about replacing anybody. It's about getting off your ass and going down to your local theatre and seeing what you can see. If we are hunting our own whale, the industry needs to go fishing too. The actors you are looking for who think this way and can do this stuff are sitting in my studio right now and working on unfunded projects with shoe-string budgets all over Dublin.

I'll miss Philip, although I never knew him. Heroin takes no prisoners. Pain of a break up of family must be horrible. Heath had to wear it too. I know for a fact I could never survive it. Artistically that ocean out there can be lonely. Sometimes you become obsessed with the whale. Sometimes you wonder why you bother and look at all the happy people on the shore and know it's all too late to go back. However we will never know what truly drove Philip to that heroin-fueled bender that ended his life. That's his business and as it is with all media, no matter how much we read about it we will never know the truth. It will always be conjecture, stabbing in the dark and hoping to hit on the truth. The essence of the man, Philip Seymour Hoffman, was never the persona he wanted us to know and see. I never knew him and so it's none of my business. He built other personae called characters for us. He was an actor.

So let's do the same. Let's look at acting.

As in my previous books, "The Beautiful Stage" and "The Art of Acting", I write these words for my students, inspired by their challenges and questions, spurred on by their insatiable desire to better themselves. I write without assistance, so please forgive my errors. I hope it is of use.

The Possible Someone

COMPLEX ACTING

So you've bought another book on acting.

Still trying to understand it? Still confused by all the arguments about it? Well this book may or may not solve that for you. What I will do is try to clarify things even more than I have in The Art of Acting. I'll give you a specific approach that works. Whether it's for you or not is up to you. Then we're going to reach for other places. These other places are quite new and require more than a redefining or a rethinking of acting. They require new definitions and new thinking and that's where we are going in this book.

A long time ago I had the rather amazing experience of teaching an advanced class that suddenly turned on me and said that it was all too much pressure to reach for the levels I was trying to push them to. As I sat in front of them, listening to them all backing each other up, nodding, affirming and closing ranks, I had a kind of epiphany. I *was* pushing them too hard and expecting far too much of them. And I realized I had to slow down and rethink the order of things, my expectations of my students and my expectations of myself. I was guilty of getting over excited.

"You're right," I said. "You don't have to do anything other that what satisfies you." The words fell out just like that. I remember them precisely.

They were a little shocked. I think, like Mamet or Meisner or other famously grumpy teachers who would otherwise have shown them the door, they expected me to defend my approach.

But in actor training the approach is only as good as the effect it has on the student. Otherwise it's little more than ego-gratification on the part of the teacher. Here were a group of my advanced students shaking their heads and throwing their hands in the air over something that I understood myself, but essentially could not explain to them. Specifically, that thing we were working on is what Stanislavski called The Threshold of the Subconscious. It's often referred to in my studio as Immersion, Abandon or Third Place. And of course it is nebulous. It's almost impossible to teach it and very difficult to invent exercises to illuminate it. It requires the actor to step up to the plate and do a few things at the same time. Hold on. Let go. Be present. Disappear.

Let's face it, when you think about it, it's ridiculous to ask anyone to broach it, and of course many will attack it and profess that it's not necessary anyway. Some flat out refuse to acknowledge its existence.

So right now you might be wondering what I'm talking about if you haven't read "An Actor Prepares" and haven't trained in a technique that has a systematized, logical progression built into it. So I will wind back. As I do, I'm going to take us through the levels of the work one step at a time and try to clarify, again, the road to artistic excellence. However, after that there's another place, a third place that you can go if you want to. But you don't have to.

After that again, there's a fourth place. This is the place where the whole idea of acting shifts into another gear and all the half-guessing, argument, cynicism and petty approaches to "being real" become utterly irrelevant. This is the place where words cease to be useful to define anything much at all. It's a place in which the actor no longer thinks things out, or even relies on instinct, or moves from one idea to another. It's a place in which the actor, in a way, forgets everything.

My estimation has always been that Stanislavski, Meisner, Strasberg, Adler and others were all in the business of simplifying acting for the actor to make it easier for them to achieve believable, truthful and interesting results. They tried to do this in very different ways using ideas that sprung from Stanislavski's work. They disagreed with each other over which of Stanislavski's ideas were right or wrong or even dangerous, but at the end of the day, simplification was the goal.

Meisner simply asked for his actors to get out of their own heads and listen to each other. If an actor can do this and know the lines by rote so that they are not pre-planning or looking ahead to the next line, there is no reason why the actor should not be completely "in the moment".

Strasberg wanted "real" emotion. He told his actors to use the emotions of their own lives and memories. Why? Because you know that they are real because you have really felt them. All you have to do is remember them, relive them and feed them into the work. Simple.

Adler trained her actors to walk and talk at the same time. Believe in the reality of the world around you and you can live truthfully in those given circumstances. Don't "act". "Do".

Of course they were all after "realism" and life-like performances and each of their techniques is absolutely right. Each one works and each one is an attempt at simplification, clarification and life-like believability; something that's convincing and not contrived. There are famous stories, and you can see video footage, of all these teachers flying into tempers and demanding results from their actors. They knew their ideas worked… for them as actors… and for some of their students, but when it didn't work, panic often set in. Of course my early work is a step off from theirs. The development of simple and effective technical tools has steered me true for a long time and helped my actors become acceptable to the palate of realistic stage and screen performance. However at a certain point that exploration of simplification hit a natural end-point for me, and the process of complication began. That realm of deep complexity has to do not with the search for realism but the search for the essence of the character as an individual human being, a complex being and further as a kind of higher form of us designed to reveal truths about the human condition within the dynamic of dramatic art. Complexity moves us into a deeper explanation of the character as an artistic subject.

Naturally I was afraid of it. It flew in the face of the simplifiers of acting. It flew in the face of effective teaching. "Make it simple for the kids. They're actors not rocket scientists." It made me afraid of being seen as impossible or difficult or egotistical. By teaching "simple" you can ensure that every actor comes along at the same pace and everyone achieves. But something in me couldn't let go of the temptation to ask tougher things of my students. All my life I've tried to learn complex things that I couldn't master such as music or quantum mechanics. Everything else in the world exists in layers of complexity including life itself. There are simple organisms and complex ones. There's basic mathematics and complex math. Why should acting be any different? Why should I be trying to simplify acting and make it a basic process only, just because all the teachers who have gone before me were doing that? Why should I assume that my students could only handle simple ideas when some, and often many of them are capable of complexity? And then I went right back to the beginning of all my study and realized that Stanislavski was not after simplification either. Early on, yes. After that he was in other worlds altogether.

There's nothing wrong with being good at the basics of something and still enjoying and succeeding at it, and often in the industries of TV, film and indeed even stage that is all that will be asked of you. However by ignoring the complexity of acting I am also neglecting the needs of those students who can reach for those more complex levels. I'm also neglecting my own intellect and the possibilities of its reaches. And worst of all I'm neglecting acting as an art form. Of all the arts, acting has the greatest potential to penetrate the human soul and humanity itself. I have an obligation to it. I didn't find it. It found me. It's asked me to help it evolve, not to be content with simplifying it, getting the students in and paying off my mortgage.

I suppose the other big question out there, hanging over the head of actor training is, "Do we need to *feel* things as actors". Can't we just block it and move like pawns around the set? The story is still being told, is it not? Let's broach this question a little later on.

To be very simplistic about it, most actor training is an attempt at achieving convincing realism preferably with emotional accessibility and this thing called "presence" as an icing on the cake. It might also take into account the voice. It's true that some actors will struggle even with these levels, but any decent teacher will get you there. If they are not, there is something wrong with one of two things: the teacher or you. Each technique's effectiveness depends on the student to whom it is being taught.

Mamet is not the only person to rant on that Stanislavski's, Meisner's, Strasberg's techniques don't work. I have heard it from my own students who have tried to train under those techniques before coming to me. But Mamet is also quick to point out that he was not a very good actor and turned his hand to writing and directing once he copped onto that truth. I've been teaching actors now for nearly twenty years and what I know for sure is this. If the teaching is not diagnostic and individual, there is little point in doing it after the fundamentals stage. Each actor is different, thinks differently and has a myriad of personal traits that affect their ability to absorb and respond to technical tools. At a fundamentals level the actor's personality, culture or history, are of little import. At the more advanced stages the teacher finds himself asking a student why something doesn't work for her and the answer is often personal. So many actors try to get themselves into the school that they think will get them connections in the business and propel them to fame. I encourage mine to look for the school that has the most diagnostic and forensic teaching and the pedagogy that they think will take them to the highest levels of which they are capable. Individual attention is the key.

For example, Stanislavski's Sense Memory tool is a very basic one designed to bring the actor closer to the imaginative truth of the Given Circumstances. Simply put, if I can smell the alcohol and smoke of this shady bar I'm meant to be in, it will help me to exist more truthfully in those circumstances even though I'm on a stage in a three-walled set and what I can actually smell is the lingering aroma of paint and a gel that's a little too hot in one of the lamps. So I take a moment and recall a similar place I've been in before. I breathe in the air of that memory using my senses, particularly my sense of smell. Soon it's as if I can actually smell it again. Maybe not literally, but on the other hand maybe. That depends on the sensory imagination of the individual actor. Either way, the tool has worked in that I now feel less like I'm in a false stage-world and more like I'm actually *there.* Whether or not you can actually smell the alcohol and smoke is not the point. The purpose of the tool is to make you feel more convincingly like you are in the fictional world of the scene so that you can behave more convincingly during the scene in this piece of hypothetical realism.

Now some actors I train find that very basic tool immensely effective. Their imaginations and abilities to immerse themselves in memories enable them to use that tool in their work with quite astonishing results. Others just *can't do it.* They can't remember the smells, or even the bar they were in. Sometimes they simply can't concentrate long enough to allow themselves to revisit that place in an in-depth way. For whatever reason the tool of Sense Memory just doesn't work for them.

Who's at fault here? No one. Not the actor, not me the teacher and certainly not Stanislavski. What needs to happen next? The diagnostic teacher needs to find the right tools to help that actor, or help to change their thinking strategies to assist them in the use of their imagination and concentration skills. Booting them out of the school or chastising their inability to absorb the idea is the stamp of a poor teacher. Freaking out when the student questions the concept and becoming defensive about the work is the mark of a teacher who has deep-seeded doubts about the technique he or she is teaching. The only exception is the case of the bone-lazy student. Bone-laziness can be treated by attempts to inspire the student, but after that there's not much any teacher can do. Nor should the teacher waste their time with such a student when diligent students could be making good use of that time.

Where tools like Sense Memory kick in, the acting teacher is asking the actor to utilize some part of their personal self; their memories and senses and imagination. But we all don't have the same kind of memory or the same kind of senses, or indeed the same kind of imagination. In the case of Emotion Memory, what a tricky landscape that must have been for Strasberg! We all feel emotions in different ways. Some are more emotionally blocked than others. Some are emotional basket cases. The truth is we are all different and if Sense Memory doesn't work for you and you are still a vigilant and intelligent actor, something else will and a good teacher will find it.

As an actor, to throw your hands in the air and proclaim that a particular tool does not work might mean that the tool doesn't work for you but can and does work for the actor sitting next to you. In fact, that actor sitting next to you probably can't understand why Sense Memory *doesn't* work for you. For that actor sitting next to you, it's as natural as breathing. So if something doesn't work, let it go. Don't dismiss it out of hand. It might come to you later, and if it doesn't there will be another way.

However there are purely logical tools that I have found all actors can use reasonably effectively. If I ask them to pursue an Objective, it would be rare to find an actor who can't do it. If I tell them to go and get a particular thing as if it is very important to them, that's an easy task to achieve. Seduce that girl. Make that tea. Fire that worker. Forget about the audience. Forget it's a play. Forget it's a fiction. Just go and do it. Easy. In the same way that Stanislavski found that this idea was able to nullify the demonstrative air of melodrama that was innate in his actors in the late nineteenth century, so too does it help me to focus my students on simple tasks and actions. The result of course is that their self-consciousness, their self-indulgence, their fear and nerves and their often-debilitating egos are neutralized or at least lessened. They realize that acting is not about them but about the character and the task that the character is carrying out. It is not about them, but about another human being's desperate need in a certain moment in its life. Acting becomes literally "doing". There's no more time for showing off, no more time for worries about how pretty I am and no more time for fear and self-consciousness. It's the acting tool that kicks open the door to concentrated, action-based performances.

The Objective, as a tool also has another very important and effective function. In fact it has several others, but the next most important thing is that an Objective can only be achieved through the other character in the scene. I can't seduce the girl by standing in a corner and acting seductively. I can only seduce the girl by going over to the girl and... well... seducing her. Whether I succeed or not is only contingent on one thing, the girl. I can do all the "character work" I want on creating the ultimate Romeo-esque character to approach that girl, but if I don't actually convince her that she should be with me, using the words of the script of course, the performance will seem dreadfully false and contrived. It will have a manufactured air about it because it is not based in real action, the action of the Objective. It doesn't matter if the result in the text is success or failure. It is the attempt that is dramatically interesting to an audience.

The Objective takes the actor's attention off himself and puts it onto the character and the character's need. Secondly it puts the actor's attention on the other character in the scene, because only through them is that Objective going to be achieved, and finally the actor begins to think about the audience, not in fearful way, but in an artistic and constructive way. To whom is this story going to be told? Will it be satisfying to them? Am I telling it "right"? This is not a wrong headspace to be in during the rehearsal process, although many might disagree. In fact it is again a thought process that takes the actor out of their self-conscious mindset and encourages them to think about things other than themselves, like the audience who are, at the end of the day, the customers.

There is no harm, even as an actor, in asking the question, "if I went to see this at the theatre or the cinema, what would I think?" Would I find this false? Would I find it contrived and annoying. Would I be bored by it? If so, why? Trust your instincts.

So the basics of the Objective and its usages changed the way actors approached their work about a hundred or so years ago. It was the one logical principal that could break the back of contrivance. I want something. I must go and get it. Forget about everything else.

The other fundamental component that was useful, but again flawed, was the idea of Given Circumstances and the actor's ability to believe in them and commit to them fully. The Given Circumstances are who you are and where you are in the scene. Believe in them as if they are real and behave according to them is the directive of Stanislavski. In the same way that a child plays a game and kicks up when mammy wants him to go and have a bath because he is so immersed in the make-believe of his game, the actor is asked to believe in a fiction and not break out of it. The actor is asked to exist completely within a public solitude and ignore any other distractions like footlights, boom mics, make-up people, etc.

Sounds simple enough, and it is. Most actors can do this. It sometimes takes a while of running improvisations to help to compel the student actor into the circumstances and make them understand that their commitment to those circumstances is essential and not up for discussion. But again ninety-eight percent of my students can go there fairly easily and without too much kerfuffle. That said some of my students find it hard to *play*. Usually these actors have been out of the game for a while and immersed themselves in some other career and are coming back to reinvigorate their talent. The problem is that they have often been in a profession that discourages play. In fact play is discouraged in children very early also. Daydreaming, which is the food for the growth of the imagination is discouraged from a very early age. The ability to simply throw oneself into a fiction with total commitment is sometimes easier said than done and can often also depend on the way the actor is feeling on a particular day. Sometimes in our busy lives I might encounter a student who is simply tired. Playing make-believe takes energy. It's the energy of children that helps them to maintain their immersion and belief in a fictional set of circumstances for so long. They can play pirates literally for an entire day. We can often find it hard to play The Merchant of Venice for a few hours. Sometimes it feels sort of embarrassing. Sometimes we are made to feel embarrassed about it. "You're an actor... so you play make-believe. I have to drive this fucking cab." "Well... Sorry about that." Some teachers denigrate belief and many other things we do naturally as actors as unnecessary, impossible, self-indulgent and pretentious. My belief is a joke. My training is a load of tosh, and things that come naturally to me are considered obsolete by some well-known acting teacher or director. I have treated my work with intellect and respect, but it is not an intellectual profession and nor is what I do respected. Oh dear. Everything I have done naturally, everything I do now, my artistic instincts and my training are considered stupid not only by people outside my profession, but by people within it too. If that's not a recipe for depression I don't know what is!

Most of us who committed ourselves to a life in this profession from an early age had to battle many obstacles, none more difficult than the disapproval of our own families, the people who are meant to care about us and encourage us the most. Of course they are usually behaving the way they are because they think they are helping and caring by explaining how only a handful of actors make any money out of it and that we are heading into a life of poverty, horror, terror and so on and so forth, and of course we smile and thank them for their advice knowing they will never understand exactly why we do what we do and that there is no point in trying to explain it to them. However it does knock us around. It often makes us feel very isolated and alone. It sometimes makes us apologetic. "Sorry for wasting the money you put into my education." And that sometimes translates into the student actor in front of me. There's a kind of guilt and shame attached to it all that prevents the actor from truly *playing*.

So lets put down a few ground rules. Playing is not something to feel ashamed about. Nor is acting. Belief is easy and opens up possibilities for specific action based on instinct and impulse. Imagination is vast and can be used in many ways. No one has a right to tell you that your use of your imagination is wrong. Emotion Memory is as natural as empathy. Characters are real and exist if we want them too. There is an arc to the character because he or she *learns from moment to moment*. Basing your creation on an intellectual idea or an artistic or historical reference is admirable and interesting. Training is good and healthy. Acting is as valid an art form as ballet and opera. And most importantly, there is a world of exploration out there in the field of acting that has not even begun yet because acting for so long has been the hostage of those who want to keep it "simple" and denigrate it. Acting... that is the Act of Acting... is not "owned" by anyone. No one teacher, actor or director can define it and hold up their definition as quintessential. Your definition is as valid as anyone else's. Your acting is just as important as anyone else's. Everybody's right and nobody's right because there is no right. Art is a journey of exploration that won't end during your lifetime or mine. The journey IS the work. The important thing is to take the journey.

You will develop as an actor from year to year as you go along in the game. Unless of course you decide that acting is playing yourself and speaking clearly. Then you'll stay just like that and that's fine too. You do not have to apologize for being an artist. It is not pretentious or arrogant. Nor is it self-indulgent to be dissatisfied and want to get better by learning new or even old approaches that you have just discovered. Many people of course don't understand art or passion for art, and like the primal animals they are, attack that which they cannot fully comprehend. Every kind of xenophobia comes from the same unfortunate trait.

To return to the point, even with the fundamental tool of Given Circumstances, the acting teacher finds himself dealing with the history and personality of the actor. Already there are blockages making themselves evident. These blockages are death to fine acting. There can be no embarrassment, no guilt, no shame, no self-consciousness, no self-absorption, no self-laceration, nothing that causes the actor to become self-concerned at the expense of those three pillars of concentration: The Character, The Other Character and The Audience. The actor must get out of his own way.

So there must be a teaching of the student on another level, and that's to do with the way they *think about acting*. Every iconic teacher since Stanislavski has done it to some extent in order to gain the trust of their students and make them look at the profession their way. "This is how I think about acting and it works. Try it and see if it works for you." On occasion through frustration or fear they lashed out at one another's approaches; Stanislavski at Chekhov, Chekhov at Stanislavski, Meyerhold at Stanislavski, Adler at Strasberg and Mamet at Meisner and Stanislavski... and Strasberg. Once this kind of punch-up starts the consideration of the student stops. That said, it is important that the teacher's approach is clear to the student. "This is *exactly* what you are getting into in this class".

Some of the most interesting people I teach are models. They find me, or their agent sends them to me because they are branching out into acting. These are people with varying levels of talent. Some have very little, and others have a lot. Some have a lot hidden beneath a public façade that they have built up for themselves over many years of modeling and hanging out at funky fashion parties. The surface is all-important. Ugliness and vulnerability are big no-nos. Beauty and confidence are the driving forces. The idea of feeling something that will make them exhibit any other impression other than supreme confidence to the world around them is very difficult. Once the basics are in place, they pursue an Objective and believe they are in a certain fictional predicament and suddenly they stop. "Oh my God!" they exclaim. "I actually felt sad then!" "Yes, I know," I reply. "No no. You don't get it. I mean actual sadness." "Yes I know," I insist, "it won't hurt you. It's just a game." "That's like MAGIC!!!"

Now that's an extreme example, but many of us do keep real feelings when acting at arm's-length. They are kind of spooky at first and there are many teachers, directors and actors including Olivier who suggest they are unnecessary or self-indulgent. So we want to adhere to the thinking of those masters too but we just can't help *feeling* while we are acting. We can't push these impulses away, no matter how hard we try. And it's odd. Let's face it, you are feeling feelings that are not your own. They have come from something fictional. You may begin to feel "like" someone else might feel, that someone of course being the character. And of course there's no magic to it, just a belief in a fiction, the pursuit of an Objective, and an unbending insistence on staying in that game without distraction. It's child's-play. It's pretty extreme child's-play, but child's-play nevertheless. "Feelings that seem real" as Stanislavski called them in "An Actor Prepares" are not, therefore, magical, but logical... in fact for most actors they are unavoidable. Then, before we know it, we find that those feelings are causing us to behave a certain way that is not the way we would behave in those circumstances if we found ourselves in them. The feelings suddenly seem to be solving the relationships between the characters, the mood of the scene and even the blocking and we follow those impulses around the space. Why throw them out? They are doing our job for us. When the actor first feels such feelings in their initial efforts on the stage or in training they naturally want to analyze them. They look inward to ask what's happening to them. That's okay, but it then must stop. The feelings must then become the compass for action and behavior. They cannot be manipulated and they cannot be used to try to manipulate the audience. They are like an invisible rudder steering the ship. The challenge is to trust that which we cannot see.

Going back to the point about personally dealing with the student actor, actor training does become, to some degree an examination of the actor him or herself, for right or for wrong. It's not quite the same as teaching math students the formulae for trigonometry and watching them do it. The actor's own baggage can often be an obstacle to achievement. Stanislavski recognized this and made the leap from these logical tools that achieved feelings, to Emotion Memory, which insisted on real feelings and forced the actor into feeling them. Lee Strasberg grabbed onto this and the Method was born. Strasberg's Method is one of the most hopelessly misunderstood things I've ever come across in any walk of life. It's apparently dangerous and irresponsible. Apparently Daniel Day-Lewis is a Method actor. Every article about him describes him as "Daniel Day-Lewis, Method actor", when from my perspective his approach is physical, not psychological and emotional. James Dean was a Method actor and so are Pacino and De Niro. Daniel Day-Lewis is something else altogether.

What we can accurately say about the Method is that it has the goal of concentrating the actor into the emotional life of her character. By doing so with incredible intensity there can be no room for superfluous distractions. The actor performs on a river on extremely intense *real* feelings and the effect is often disarming. However the various suggestions and claims that the Method is all about emotional masturbation and uncontrolled emotional borsch are a mystery to me. Unless someone is teaching the Method in a very wrong way, the logic of Objectives and a belief in Given Circumstances and the action of the scene are still the all important starting points. Therefore, as in Stanislavski, emotion is the result of events, of things happening to the character. You cannot start with the character's emotion until something has happened to the character. Otherwise it doesn't make sense. Simply put, you can't cry for the sudden death of your mother in the scene before she's died. There must be a trigger for emotion; her sudden death. Otherwise it is grounded to nothing. Method attempts to prepare the actor for the emotion that is to come, to make those emotions accurate for the telling of the story, and this work is done using specific exercises and even more specific rehearsals.

Strasberg's Emotion Memory exercise is designed to sensitize the actor. To what end? To break down the blockages the actor has to being able to feel feelings on behalf of a character within a fiction. Once those gates are open, the actor is open to being able to access great floods of feeling. Therefore, on this level, Strasberg's work is diagnostic and deals intimately with the personality and life of the individual actor.

So what's the point of having "real" feelings? The point is that feelings often dictate our behavior in life. As such, the character's behavior might (and probably will) be dictated by the way they are feeling. The *quality* of how things are done is often determined by feelings. You make a cup of tea differently if you have just won the lottery to the way you make it when you've just scraped your doggy off the underside of a car. You can make a surface, generalized guess about what those feelings are if you like, and then try to pretend to be sad or confused or jealous or whatever, but more often than not that pretending is simply not convincing. Why? Because it is general. It is not specific to the actual thing that has happened to the character, to their circumstances and to their person. Feelings therefore can be used as a driving force to help to discover the character's truthful behavior. Often that behavior can be surprising, or even seem odd.

Allow me to redefine three terms here. Firstly "emotions" are states of feeling that we can name. Sadness, guilt, jealousy, joy. The thing is, we all behave differently when we feel these things. For example, guilt may cause one character to confess and another to clam up while another might jump ship for France. It all depends on the individual. "Feelings" however are not as definable in words, but much more useful for actors. I have these feelings towards this woman. I can't name them; lust, love, caring or perhaps a mixture of all three. Although we can't define them we can get a very real *sense* of them. I like to call these "sensations" because the word "feelings" is often misunderstood and generalized and thought of as another word for emotions. Also sensations are physical and strike at the core of a part of your body. Feelings are softer and I think too tentative. A sudden sensation while acting that you cannot define in one simple word is a gold nugget. It will dictate your behavior. A sensation moves you both physically and emotionally. It also disallows you the luxury of trying to define it using one word and then accidentally falling into the trap of playing a generalized and perhaps clichéd idea of it. Sensations are often a very immediate mix of many different emotions or feelings. They are much more useful especially when we start to delve into the more advanced usages of Multiple Objectives.

The way Hamlet behaves in that play is befuddling for many actors. Why does he talk the way he talks? Why does he treat Polonius and Ophelia in the way he does? Why does he walk and read? Why does he throw himself in her grave after essentially abusing his girlfriend? It is arguable that his feelings are motivating him to behave in a certain odd way. How can we know what those feelings are until we have embodied the truth of the man's circumstances and desires? We can't. So we try to actually experience his world and his predicament. We walk through his actions as prescribed in the play. Then, with a little bit of insistence and imagination we begin to feel feelings that seem real. During rehearsals, as our feet become firmer, those feelings become specific, physical sensations that we cannot define. We then let those sensations dictate our impulses. We let the sensations solve as much as they can; the blocking, the tone, the atmosphere and the behavior. If we have felt something similar to those sensations in our own experiences, it is natural for us to call on them. But we don't have to either. Soon we realize that we are following powerful sensations that are not our own. We find we are looking at the world around us through someone else's eyes and responding to it through someone else's way. At this point we have a pretty well formed character. We understand why Hamlet is doing what he's doing, but we could never write an academic essay on it. It's not necessary. Our sensations, physically, have become our compass.

There's nothing mysterious, occult or dangerous about any of this. It's just a way of thinking about acting that has been proven to work... for some.

Stanislavski's notion of "if"; what "if" this was me in this situation, What "if" these things happened to me? How would I feel? How would I behave? How do *I* deal with these Given Circumstances? How do *I* pursue this Objective? becomes obsolete at a certain point in this process. But it's not a bad place to start. You have to start somewhere. Pretty quickly, however, you will look at that text and realize that you would not behave in the way Hamlet does in that play. Then you are in a tricky place, trying to understand Hamlet from your own perspective. You have to let yourself go. You have to release the "I". You have to jettison the "me" in order to let someone else in. The obvious progression is, "how does *the character* deal with these circumstances? How would Hamlet behave? How would Hamlet feel? These questions were broached by Michael Chekhov as he moved towards the imagination and away from the logical progressions of Stanislavski. However these too have their limits. Actors who try to formulate how Hamlet would behave often create performances that seem to say, "Look at how I've formulated Hamlet's behavior!" There's a self-referential nature to such performances that is still irksome. Further again now, we are beginning to ask the greater questions in more specific ways for example, "What does Hamlet mean to the audience?" "What does Hamlet mean to humanity?" And from there we ask how the actor in the process can encapsulate the answers to those questions within the acting and the performance itself. These are no longer questions for directors, academics and dramaturgs alone. Can these questions lead an actor to make certain choices that are beyond the immediate pale of the action, perhaps creating metaphor or symbolism in the acting itself? Can the actor transcend the pettiness of stardom and the indulgent nature of performance, the ego of searching for the quintessential, and lend himself fully to the true search for a new and exciting Hamlet? Can the actor be more than a pawn being moved around by a director? Can the actor be allowed to be an artist? Can the actor be allowed to penetrate his own humanity to tap the well of Hamlet's? And the contradiction then goes, can the actor let Hamlet come through a greater consciousness without a guiding hand on it?

Who is Hamlet anyway?

Some say there is no character. Others conversely suggest that there is no actor… or that the less of the actor there is present in the performance the better, and of course this has led to yet another distracting argument. It's where a huge division happened in actor training. Michael Chekhov and Vsevelod Meyerhold both departed from Stanislavski on this point. Yes, they also had reservations about the use of the actor's own emotions and memories, suggesting that such an approach was dangerous. But all of this discourse stemmed from the issue of the actor playing himself and relying on himself as opposed to the character, using his own emotional life rather than discovering the individual inner-life of the character. Whose story is it anyway, the actor's or the character's? Now however, these ideas are antiquated. No matter where you choose to search for the character or how you choose to define what a character is, the search is for the story of the character, the meaning of the character, the meaning *in* the character and the higher truths that the character represents.

The Hollywood Star System is not the first star system. Something similar had been going on for a couple of hundred years before Stanislavski. Star actors like David Garrick and Elenora Duse drew huge audiences. People slept in queues in the streets for days to get a ticket. They were not coming to see Hamlet. They were coming to see David Garrick playing Hamlet. Today we do not go to the Mission Impossible films to see the character. I couldn't even tell you what the character's name is in the Mission Impossible movies. And nor do I care. We are going to see Tom Cruise playing that dude and we are going to see what cool new stuff he has done with special effects and action sequences that will blow us away even more than the last Mission Impossible movie did. And everybody knows it. Why do you think it is so hard for you to get a major job as an actor? Because there is a star system. An actor is chosen by some production company somewhere and someone in that company decides they are going to make this actor the next big star in order to make money from the "product" of that actor. Some very rich person somewhere is amused or titillated by a certain actor and basically places a bet that millions of other people will be too. It sometimes succeeds and sometimes fails. You're not being offered those big roles because someone has not chosen you to be their next big thing. You can't make them money. Audiences won't prick up their ears when they hear your name. You do not command a fan base. This "chosen one" will be offered that part. This "chosen-one" may be a good actor. He or she may not be. I personally don't think Tom Cruise or Keira Knightly or Orlando Bloom are particularly "good" actors, but people flock to see them by the millions, making a lot of people a lot of money in the process. It's business and the audience is entertained by it, so who's to criticize it? It's simply my opinion and my own preference about what I like to see on the cinema screen. It's my own definition of good acting and it is no more or less valid than anyone else's.

On the other hand, I do think Daniel Day-Lewis is a good actor and in his work I see a concerted effort to play the character as opposed to settling for playing himself. Furthermore, and this may be just my imagination, I have a suspicion that Daniel is reaching for something else again, over and above the playing of a character. I notice his very specific choices of projects and they don't seem to be choices he is making from his wallet. You can never disguise the actor. That's obvious. Nobody's trying to fool anyone. However you can choose to penetrate and expose the essence of the character in order to more effectively tell the character's story. If you wish to do that, you, your personality, your idiosyncrasies, your gestures, your way of thinking, your way of feeling, your attitudes and opinions, your voice and the essential thing that is you needs to step out of the way and allow something else to step in. It is a very selfless and rather affirming process. And most importantly, if you intend to work on this level, you need to accept that the character exists and exists as fully and absolutely as you or I or anyone else you see walking down the street. You have to make the solid imaginative leap that this person is *real* and your job is to become them; not to imitate them or mimic them or use their words while being yourself and showing off, but actually embody their ways and means, their thoughts and feelings and all the ins and outs of their personality, idiosyncrasies and traits. If they are an historical character, there they are. Lucky you. If not, your imagination goes to work and creates a fully formed vision of this other life called "the character". That is not lying and it is not an attempt to fool the audience. It is an effort to penetrate to the core of the character and reveal their essence rather than showing off your own. That starts to happen when you're about two pages into reading the script. It's not just words on a page anymore. It's imagined lives in an imagined world. As an actor who is an artist, you are already feeling yourself being drawn into the character as if stepping into a room you have never been in before, exploring it for the first time. You are not working out how you are going to bust it up with a sledge hammer in order to change it to suit yourself or use it to show off some side of your own personality. You are seeking the truth of the room itself.

And here's the rub. Being Tom Cruise helps Tom Cruise to do his job of pulling in millions to see his movies and make himself and his people very wealthy. Daniel Day-Lewis being Daniel Day-Lewis helps Daniel to have the options of playing the most interesting roles out there. But once he makes a decision, does his work and the thing goes into the cinema, being Daniel Day-Lewis is an encumbrance to his communication with the audience. It's something he has to get his audience past.

Why bother, I hear you say? That sounds like a terrible and seemingly ridiculous amount of hard work. What's the point when all the audience want to see is you being you anyway? Well there are two reasons for doing it in my estimation. Number one is that I don't want to be splashed all over a cinema screen for millions of people to see. I don't want to have "me" up there. Why would I want that? That's not what acting is all about to me. My voice and body and personality are my own and are private things that I might choose to share with my friends and family. I'm not telling the story of me, I'm telling the story of this other life that I've read about in this script. The second reason is that creating a fully formed character is not hard work to me at all. It is *fun*! I find it a joy! I also find it an artistic process and that thrills me. I find it an incredible journey to the bottom of the sea or the center of the Earth. It's exciting. It feeds my curiosity to explore another life other than my own. It helps me to get out of my head, a head I have to live in all day everyday in the difficult life-long effort of being me. Here's an opportunity to be someone else for a period of time. And not only is it another life, it is another life fraught with theatrical and dramatic ups and downs! Where's the hard work? To suggest its hard work is akin to a child pulling down the harness on a rollercoaster and sighing, "well here we go. This is going to be a lot of hard work." If you feel like that about it, get off the rollercoaster and go home. There are literally thousands of others who want your seat.

Yes, sometimes that journey into the life of someone else is difficult. Sometimes you just don't seem to be able to *see* them or understand them. Sometimes you hit a wall or a block of some kind. Sometimes you get distracted while trying to see the world out of their eyes and behave as them and you get frustrated and have to stop and take a break and try again. Sometimes you go a little too far and you end up living in that completely absorbing world and forget yourself for a little too long. But that's rare and even when it happens, a little fright is had and the real world is all still there and everything is ok. You're not going to need a psychiatrist and you won't end up in an asylum if your mind plays a trick on you that you are someone you are not for a little while. In the same way that a 3D movie might make you think the train is going to smash you in the face, you might flinch and get a shock, but it's just an image. It's all a mirage and it's all just a game, no matter how real it all might seem.

That said, if it seems that convincing to you, it will more than likely seem that convincing to the audience. That's not an absolute certainty, and we'll discuss that a bit later too. However if you are undistracted by your own crap, absorbed in a fully formed world, you are going to do an incredibly good job of telling that character's story *as* them. The audience will suspend their disbelief and, although they know you are an actor, they will let that go and allow themselves to be absorbed by the progression of the story and the revelation of the character's essence. If it is not convincing and enthralling to the audience, something has probably gone a bit wrong. That's when a good director will step in and ask you a few questions about your choices and your steps to getting where you have gotten. Your director is not being rude. Your director is trying to isolate exactly where that wrong turn was taken so that you can both backtrack and turn the right way back at that juncture. Even Daniel Day-Lewis had a moment of this nature during the shooting of "There Will Be Blood". It's part of the work.

Let's not get into this in too much depth yet and stick to the point. Once again, the individual actor needs to ask the question of herself, "What do I want to do?" What kind of actor do you want to be? Why are you in the game in the first place? As a teacher it is part of my job to encourage an honest response to these questions purely so that I can teach you in the best way I can. There is no point in me trying to teach you a very complex concept if you have no interest in learning anything complex. Your acting teacher must know who you are and what you want. Otherwise they will end up with a student in front of them who hasn't got his lines down after three weeks and he has to look at that actor and tell the truth, and truth is that that actor just doesn't want to be an actor. He wants to be something else and has been given the wrong impression about acting. On a more complex level, a certain actor may start to deal with real and palpable sensations and run a mile. Another actor will say intently that they want to tackle the advanced stuff of character creation, but in the end can't get out of her own head and how her hair is looking that day. The training is all there, but the actor must come to the party too. They don't have to change who they are or how they behave, but they have to understand that certain thought-processes and behaviors are not conducive to achieving within the creative process of the work at some levels.

I can see why Meisner was grumpy sometimes. He threw the same tools at all his actors and tried to make them all selfless, open listeners. He had varying degrees of success. That's because some of his students were naturally predisposed to those behaviors, some could change through the process of his exercises to become more like that, and others just could not understand why he wanted them to look at the person opposite and repeat over and over that they were wearing a blue shirt. They were wrapped up in themselves, resistant to change and learning. They hadn't come to learn. They had come to be reassured that they were "good". Of course the more of that reassuring you do in a technique like Meisner, the more self-absorbed the actor becomes. It's a downward spiral of naval gazing when the energy of the actor is being encouraged out and away from themselves, not in towards themselves. So Meisner didn't encourage them where encouragement wasn't due. He just showed them the door and hence became known as a great teacher to those who were predisposed, or changed themselves to respond to his technique, and a bollocks to those he had no patience for.

So now we are in the world of dealing with technical tools that are solid and understandable, but will be digested in different ways by different actors depending on the parameters of their own personalities and how much or how little they can set those personality peculiarities aside. As we go along, ask yourself how you are responding to these ideas and how they might inform your acting.

Now, it's time to dig into things that are sometimes called "deeper", sometimes called "better", sometimes called "more advanced" and sometimes called "more sophisticated". But what's most important to me is that they make acting more wondrous and enjoyable for my actors and students.

The Possible Someone

IMMERSIVE ACTING

One day when I was very young I was acting and found myself immersed in a fictional world so fully that I completely forgot who I was and what reality was. I was flowing down a river of rapids. I could steer it, but couldn't stop. No matter how much I might have *wanted* to be distracted or brought out of it, I couldn't have. It was an amazing trip.

From that point on I have wanted to share that feeling with people and so began a life-long process of penetrating the nature of this somewhat mysterious phenomenon. It's not easy. There's the risk that people will look at you like you're some kind of crazy person. So, as an actor you stop trying to explain it to family and friends and interviewers and media. However, as a teacher, surrounded by other actors, there is a *knowledge* not a *belief* among those actors sitting in front of you that that world of immersion is out there. It exists and they want to know about it. They want to know how they can get there, or if their mental and physical make-up is such that they can, or if their talent is such that they can. They want to know what the hell that place is. How and why does it exist? The development of my teaching has been focused on this force and every exercise and every rehearsal is bent towards it in one form or another. So perhaps I can't explain it to you, but I can *teach* it.

I have experienced it enough myself to know it exists and have heard it reported from enough actors to know it has been found by many others also, so I have no need to convince anyone of its existence anymore or justify myself or the work in some way. It just is. To describe it, I have previously tried to explain it as the place of pure-form inspiration that the painter or writer gets into when the work of art seems to begin to create itself... when the arm and hand and the brush in that hand seem to be working independently of the artist. Stanislavski called it Subconscious. I like this word for a number of reasons. So lets start with that. Yes it's mysterious, but it's not as mysterious as some might have led you to believe it is. And what's wrong with a bit of mystery in our ever more functional and logical lives anyway?

The subconscious is something we all have. In life we don't somehow "act out" moving from here to there. We just move from here to there. Often we can do several things at the same time because of that "subconsciousness". We can make a cup of tea, hold a conversation about something quite important and check that the cakes are not burned in the oven at the same time. We don't even think literally about each step of what we are doing, we seem to just be able to do them and each one of those tasks holds a greater or lesser degree of importance at a given moment and we trundle along.

Imagine then, being able to exist like that, in character. The problem of course is that the very nature of subconscious behavior is that we are not thinking about it when we are doing it. How can you consciously behave subconsciously? You can't. What you can do, however, is work *towards* subconscious behavior. We behave subconsciously in life because we know ourselves, our gestures, our movement and our physicality so intimately that we do not have to think about them as we move through our everyday existence. Can we achieve this level of knowledge of our character? Can the character know itself and its ways so well that we can let them behave without our manipulation of them, even though it is our body, brain and facility that are being used by the character as it moves through the play or film?

Following the journey towards realism that Stanislavski took, we look for the Objective and the Given Circumstances in the script. Yes, they are there, as they are in every moment of our "real" lives. We are on the right track if we can therefore believe in those Given Circumstances and pursue that Objective. We are behaving in character as we would in life. However, in life we do not think of the line in the script coming up. We do not have footlights and an audience in front of us. We do not have a camera and a boom mic pointed at us. In life we do things subconsciously, like riding a bike. We just get on and pedal. We don't think logistically about the mechanics of pushing the pedals around and keeping balance. As such the Subconscious in acting achieves a state where the actor is behaving *in character subconsciously*. There are no distractions, no questionings, no concerns about the completeness of the work, no self-consciousness on the part of the actor. The Objective is being pursued without thinking of the logistics of what it is and how vehemently it should be being pursued. The Given Circumstances are not being believed with effort, they are assumed to be true. They are not even considered as something that needs to be negotiated anymore. I simply *am* on a spaceship. I might have to do my homework as an actor to *get there*. Once that's done however, I don't have to do any work to simply *be* there.

Now what's the point of this "subconsciousness" thing? Is it going to make the performance I'm giving more believable than if I simply pretend and go through the actions in a conscious, choreographed way, making them look as natural as possible? Perhaps. Perhaps not. Why bother is answered personally. You bother because you can and because you want to and because you think it might be useful for the telling of the story. Conversely you don't bother if you don't think its necessary.

As we know, in filmic realism it is important to maintain the most believable performance as possible. In life we do things subconsciously, so if we can achieve that *in character* we have a little bit better chance of achieving that total naturalness of behavior. Sure, you can pretend it and pretend it well and get away with it. Perhaps this is what Olivier was talking about when he criticized Hoffman for getting himself into a physical state during Marathon Man. He said, "Why don't you try acting?" What he was really saying was, "Why don't you try pretending?" And why not? It's not as physically taxing as staying awake for a long time and running around the block four times, or whatever Hoffman was supposed to have done. The problem with pretending, and this is only an opinion, is that it leaves open the possibility of that contrivance coming across as contrived or unnatural on the camera. It also diminishes the possibility of something accidental and extraordinary happening. In my experience of teaching, when an actor pretends to be exhausted, he remembers what exhaustion feels like and tries to replicate it. He demonstrates that exhaustion for his audience, huffing and puffing, hands on the knees, bent over, and so on and so forth. All of the physical cliché's of exhaustion come in. However he tends to speak faster than he could if he were truly exhausted. From there we have to repair the holes in the truth of the performance. Slow down. No, he wouldn't talk like that. No, that bit with the feet isn't believable. You're over-doing it. Take a bit off it. It becomes a long process of finding the best "pretending". If he is actually exhausted, he does all sorts of interesting things. His speech is believable. He must pause to catch his breath. Instead of putting his hands on his knees, he puts them on his head and stretches up. A pain strikes him in his side. A stitch. He has to deal with that as he plays the scene. Not only is it believable, it's utterly convincing because it is true. It's also utterly convincing because he is dealing with that exhaustion *truly*. He is doing things subconsciously, pausing, moving, speaking, sitting down, sweating. All of these things now seem to *work* and I have much less work to do myself of searching for the convincing imitation of exhaustion that we were trying to hack out before.

If realism is the goal, then why not be real? If we can't be real, then lets look at trying to create the best imitation. I wouldn't expect one of my actors to take heroin, for example. But if they are making a cup of tea, lets actually make it. Lets not act it out. And by actually making it and focusing on the Objective in an immersed state, we have the possibility of something extraordinary happening. Maybe the tea won't get made at all. Maybe the scene will change and be enhanced by an immersed performance.

That said, realism is not always the goal. Some forms of theatre and film require representation and stylization. These are languages that take us away from the "real truth" of the performance and into another kind of abstract, metaphorical or higher truth. These forms also require the in-depth understanding that the actor has of his body. However that body is to be used in these forms in different ways.

The Subconscious is *interesting* and *fun*. It might hold the keys to a moment of performance that is accidental and excellent in that it enhances the narrative in a way that neither the writer nor director had previously conceived. The actor truly becomes a part of the artistic process. That which is potentially accidental is potentially risky. So why put the performance at risk? Risk means walking the edge of disaster. Risk is the act of putting everything on the edge of the highest peak in order to be at the highest point, with the possibility there that the whole lot might fall off the edge.

Again, we don't have to do that, but risky theatre is interesting theatre. It's rarely seen and when it happens the established audience of that theatre throws a hissy fit because they didn't see the safe thing they were used to seeing at "their" theatre. However if we never take risks, the art of theatre-making simply cannot evolve. We have no choice. We have to risk getting a bad review from a critic who didn't get it or losing some of our audience because their palate needs to develop with us.

Back to the subconscious and immersion. How do we get there? For the first time in actor training, there are definable tools for getting there.

First of all we must live in the realms of The Learning Character. This concept essentially is that the character knows nothing until it happens to them. The *trick* of course is that the actor knows everything. The actor has read the script and learned the words. But the character has not. The character knows nothing; not the words, not the actions, not the surprises that are coming, not his death at the hands of Laertes and the king, nothing at all.

The first step then is to take a leap out of Meisner's book and learn the lines by rote. Get them in, know them like the "Hail Mary" or the alphabet or whatever you have had drummed into your head. You don't rattle off the alphabet worrying that you will lose the lines. You don't look ahead to the next letter. It is just there. You don't even have to actively trust yourself that you will get to "Z". You just subconsciously know you will.

How do you do that? How do you learn by rote? In the same way that you learned the alphabet or the "Hail Mary". You go over it and over it a million times. You don't try to emphasize a particular letter or phrase. You don't look for what emotions you might represent on a certain phrase at a certain stage. You just learn it. Though the "Hail Mary" is a beautiful tract of poetry and holds great emotional meaning to the faithful, one can still rattle it off like the alphabet anytime if one has been brought up Catholic. You can rattle it off without meaning, just for the words themselves.

When you begin to learn a tract of text or script, initially forget about the other character's lines. Just learn yours. Learn them one after the other as if there were no lines in between and your lines are a kind of disjointed monologue or an itemized list. In doing this you will notice a logical progression of thought in your own character. How does my character get from this thought to the next? He is spurred on by something that has either happened or been said in between those lines. The progression between the two lines makes no sense without the thing in between. For example:

John: I'm going to the pub.

Jane: Don't go to the pub. You're drinking far too much lately.

John: Keep your judgments to yourself.

I'm John so I learn two lines: "I'm going to the pub" and "Keep your judgments to yourself". I don't need to know what Jane says to me in between. It is clear that she must have said something significant for me to go from "I'm going to the pub" to "Keep your judgments to yourself". You learn your lines like a list, by rote. Then you rattle them off to yourself as many times as you can in that list in that order. Do not just sit at a table, put down your head and learn them. Move. Once you essentially have them, rattle them off with the radio on, dancing. Clean out the dishwasher and rattle them off. Pick up the dog shits and rattle them off. Rattle them off while you're taking a shower. Why? Because you are saying them while doing things that you normally do subconsciously. As such the lines too will settle into your subconscious. Soon you will not be worried about what the next one is. It will come to you as surely as "M" follows "L" in the alphabet. Learning this way has another advantage. Once you are in front of the other actor in rehearsals, you will have no preconceived way of delivering the lines. You have learned them while doing things subconsciously and while doing things that could have distracted you and thrown you. Yet you could still rattle them off. As such, when you stand in front of the other actor, what they do will not throw you. It will be a surprise as all things are in life because we don't know they are coming and we have to deal with them in that moment in real time. Better again, *what they do will dictate what you do*. You don't even have to think ahead to that line "Keep your judgments to yourself". You know it is there. You say, "I'm going to the pub". She says, "Don't go to the pub. You're drinking far too much lately". And it is the tone and quality of Jane's line that will decide, *in the moment*, the tone and quality of "Keep your judgments to yourself." As such, the conversation is real in the sense that, as in life, one thing follows another. Nothing is prepared in advance. Even if we rehearse in our heads how a certain confrontation might go with another person, it never quite happens that way. Why? Because we can rarely predict what the other person is going to say. Even more rarely can we predict how they are going to say it. And even more rarely again can we predict how we are going to really feel in that confrontation. We say to ourselves, "well I'm going to be stoical and calm" and we end up screaming our heads off, or we think we will end up losing the rag and surprisingly come out having behaved stoically and calm.

Now let's be very clear what all this means at the actual point of learning the lines. When I tell actors to learn them by rote and not to preordain how they are going to say the line or what emotion they are going to attach to it, some of them misinterpret that as a directive to not feel any kind of emotional attachment to the line as an actor. Trying to learn lines that you *don't care about* is incredibly difficult if not impossible. It's much easier to learn a line that inspires you than one that does not. *O for a muse of fire that would ascend the brightest heaven of invention.* I mean, how can you not be stunned by the beauty of that first line of Henry V? It's wondrous! I'm not asking you to become detached from the excellence or cleverness of the writing. Quite the opposite. Fall in love with it as part of your first acquaintance with the text. What I'm asking is that you don't decide to do it "scary" or do it "light" or do it "evil" and learn it as only "scary", "light" or "evil" so that you are unable to adapt to another way. Learn the words so you don't have to think about how you will say them till you're in front of me, your director and together we work out the best way to tell the story, starting with those words. In fact, know them so that you don't have to think about them at all.

Rote is Meisner's word. When I was growing up and learning lines or songs or music my teachers used to say, "learn it off by heart". Perhaps this is a better and nicer way to say it. Learn it so you don't have to look at the words or the notes anymore or indeed even think about them when you're performing. And learn them with your heart so that they not only go into your head, but into your heart. Own them.

Let's say now that you can run the lines by rote with another actor. The second time you run it you will not be able to help but feel some kind of sensation when Jane says, "Don't go to the pub. You're drinking far too much lately." You notice that the quality of your own line of "Keep your judgments to yourself" is beginning to be imbued with a quality that has been born of the reactive sensation that you are having to Jane's protestation. It's beginning to sound like a real conversation because the reactions are genuine, unplanned and based on sensations. They are not being manipulated. Now, lets take a look at the rest of the play and the characters' backstories. Let's imagine that John is going to the pub each night to watch football, but is also engaging in flirtations with a single woman who also frequents the bar. Let's imagine he has been doing this five nights a week and on the other two nights he remains detached from his partner. Let's imagine John and Jane have not made love for two months. We will go into this in more detail later, but imagine that you understand all that intellectually, let it drop down into your system so that you "feel" the sensations of that inner mess and then run the scene again. The learning of the lines is a distant technical necessity. The lines now mean nothing. They just sit on top of the sensations bounding around within the characters.

As a slight sideline, this kind of learning makes auditions and screen tests an awful lot easier. You just don't know what the set up is going to be in there so there's no point in trying to predict it. You could be in front of a panel, or not. The director might be there, or perhaps only the casting director. You could be on your own or sent in with someone else. There could be a reader opposite you or another actor who will be playing the other role. It's all up in the air. However, if you can run your lines while picking up dog shits, you can run them anywhere, no matter what alien circumstances present themselves.

In fact, let me extend an arm a little further on this at the risk of confounding some. You should not be looking for the line before you say it. Nor should you be "on the line" with your character's thought. Indeed your character's thought should come just *after* the line, and preferably come freely and not manipulated by the actor.

"To be or not to be, that is the question". Out it comes like spilled liquid. Then Hamlet realizes the thesis he has encapsulated… and expands. I'll discuss this more later on.

Trying to predict how a scene is going to turn out on stage or in front of the camera before at least rehearsing in an organic way with the other actor is just as pointless. Many directors improvise around the conflict in the scene before pinning the lines on it. Stanislavski did this too. Why? Because improvisation robs the actor of pre-planned decisions. It makes everything fresh and new and *in the moment* because the character has to think and react in real time to altered circumstances. You can only control your character to a certain degree. Once all your homework is done and they are in that moment, suddenly they turn over a chair and you get to the end of the scene and wonder what on earth happened. The character happened. You apologize to the director and the other actor and both of them know that that was the take that will be used. You can't plan it.

Okay. We're leaping ahead slightly. The point here is, how the hell can you expect any kind of organic, subconscious behavior to occur in the character when the actor is searching around in the empty tin can of his head for the next line while trying to say the present line in some kind of convincing way? It's a hopeless exercise and it is evident in the poorest acting. Actors come to me after such a show and say, "Oh Dave! We were "under-rehearsed"! It was such an awful feeling." Under-rehearsed? You mean you didn't know your lines well enough to behave organically and communicate with the other actor on the stage. There's no point in blaming the director. The director can't learn your lines for you. Bad direction is when the staging and nuances and balances don't add up or when the vision doesn't congeal or whatever. Making it blatantly obvious that you are searching for the next line is the fault of the actor. The director has his own job to do.

Great rugby players play with their club team, then get thrown into a provincial team and pushed out onto the pitch, then suddenly they are playing for their country and they have never played with the player next to them that they are meant to be passing the ball too. They get in as much training as they can and pass the ball to each other as much as they can to get to know the pace and rhythm of the other guy. It doesn't take very long when you are working at that level because they both have the same language of Rugby. They both have the skills. Really they could probably go straight out there and just do it. Then they do get out there in front of ninety thousand people with a wall of monsters in front of them. But the coach has a game plan and they have a few ideas about how they are going to get by them. They have never questioned that they know what they are doing. They have never questioned their skills. Every director in the professional sphere *assumes* that the actors they are going to be working with will come in with razor-sharp skills. As such the cut and thrust between actors who are that skillful will steer the work and make it grow. They both have the same language of Acting. Imagine sticking some schmo into the Irish Rugby team who has never kicked a ball before? And people still try to tell me that training is unnecessary.

On the same note, if a particular rehearsal goes very well, the temptation is to say, "Ok. That's the one. Let's do that." And more than likely you can't repeat it to the same level of satisfaction. Of course you can't. Try having a great night out that seemed to happen organically where you met someone who just blew you away and you talked till four in the morning, and then go out the next weekend and try to do it again. It can never happen the same way ever again. There might be other good nights, equally as good even, but never the same. The performance must always remain organic. That's preferable. But that said, if you revert to a very good imitation of a great run of it you had before, that's not bad either, just nowhere near as satisfying. The audience may not know the difference. That said, they do know. They always know. They might not be able to articulate it, but the danger of the organic performance is either there or it is not. If it is not, there's always a kind of void.

Let's wind back slightly to the over-throwing of the chair issue. It can't be papered over. Often an actor will see a moment on screen or stage that was utterly organic and they will decide to attempt such an organic moment by pre-planning it. "Right. At that line I will turn over the chair in rage." This will not and can never work. It is pre-planned it is not organic. It will certainly come across as contrived and manipulated. You cannot plan any kind of response of this nature. It happens purely by nature in the moment of the performance. If it does not happen, it is probably correct for the story for it *not* to happen.

Method acting has been terribly misconstrued in this way. There is a generalization that one must exhibit heightened emotional borsch, otherwise it is wrong. This happens because actors see great actors on stage and screen hitting these moments of high emotional intensity and think that that is what they must achieve, otherwise they will be somehow "wrong". The containment of emotion is often far more powerful than the revelation of it. Look at Strasberg himself in The Godfather II. The containment of emotion is almost stifling and utterly enthralling. The judgment of these moments comes down to the character being played. Does my character let their emotions out? Maybe I would, but do they? Does my character restrain their emotions? Maybe I would, but perhaps they cut loose and let fly.

What if the writer has prescribed an emotional response in the stage or screen directions? Two answers here. Number one, good writers rarely if ever do it these days. They used to so you will find it in Chekhov, Ibsen and even as late as Williams and Miller. So number two, if they do prescribe such a moment, there will be an inherent build-up to that point written into the action of the script. If the actor has done their homework the right way they will have no other option but to cry, weep, laugh, throw the chair or whatever has been prescribed in the directions. The writer is simply giving you a hint that that is the where you should be at emotionally. If you're not, go back and look again at the build-up. You have probably missed something. If it's Arthur Miller you can be pretty sure he hasn't made a mistake.

So we are talking about those things that must be in place if you have any hope of being immersed in the character's world enough to walk this threshold of the subconscious. Obviously learning your lines by rote is one very basic one. If you're looking ahead for the lines, you can't be in the moment. That makes sense. So what is that exactly? It's a distraction. A distraction from "the moment." What else distracts us when we are acting? Well the environment of course. It's a false environment. On the stage you have fake sets, foot lights beaming up at you and sometimes several hundred people looking at you from a dark abyss. On screen you have a camera pointed at you, maybe two dozen people doing a myriad of jobs flitting around you, putting marks on the floor by your feet, powdering your face, taking light readings, adjusting your costume, measuring for depth with a long tape, fixing a radio-mic to your belt, bumping your head with a boom-mic and so on and so forth. Now when "action" is called, that's all supposed to settle down so you can play the scene, but that doesn't always happen. And if you're just playing a small role, you are hardly in a position to tell the director that you need more quiet. You can try, but really if there's a lot of farting around and joke-telling happening, you're going to feel like one big yangar if you put your foot down and put a stop to it. On the other hand if you're Christian Bale or Daniel Day-Lewis, you have a little more clout and can insist on an environment of concentration, and if you don't get it, you can rip someone a new one for it.

When you arrive on a professional film set for the first time, or work in the professional theatre and have come from the hard slog of profit share shows and student films, you will feel like you are being treated like royalty. Why is that? It's not because everyone thinks you're a god, so get your head out of the clouds. It's because everyone is trying to create an environment where you will feel comfortable and *not distracted* so you can deliver the best performance they can get from you. You will have noticed that you got a wake-up phone call from the assistant director and a driver picked you up and drove you to the set. That's not because they want to treat you like a star by providing you with a chauffeur. It's to ensure that your ass is on the set on time, because time is money and if your own alarm didn't go off or your stupid car gets a flat tyre, the whole day is screwed from the start. You will have your own trailer or dressing room where you can go to keep warm, lie down, take a moment or two and get yourself ready for the performance which is often a moment of magic in film and a tour de force for a couple of hours on the stage. You will be fed three hot meals a day. Between takes people will ask if you'd like coffee or water. They will throw a keep-warm jacket on you if it's cold. Anything that distracts could be death to the shot. On a truly professional set, you will be able to walk away from people and they won't think you're being rude. Extras will have been told not to speak to you, and if they do they ask your permission first before striking up a conversation, not because you are superior to them or anyone else, but to make sure they're not accidentally breaking your concentration.

The point is, if everyone else is so intent on ensuring you're in the right headspace to play that role, you had better be bloody sure you are too. You'd better have done your homework and you had better have a technique that can remove distractions, concentrate you and achieve high quality results. Yes everyone has a job to do on that film set, but for the most part they are technical jobs. Everyone also recognizes that there is someone else there that is trying to do something that is other than technical. That person is the actor and to some extent the director and the director of photography and possibly the make-up artist depending on the production, but it's the actor whose head is going to end up on that screen. The thing that these people are trying to achieve is based on technical knowledge, but flows to something that is a little less tangible but certainly real, called art. It only happens if the technical work is right. From there the "talent" of those artists can be allowed to shine through. Because no one fully understands what artistic talent is or where it comes from, it's probably best to create an environment where those artists are not distracted and feel comfortable. That's the thinking.

So a lot of people are trying their best (usually) to reduce the impact of that distracting environment on you as much as they can. What can you do to assist? Obviously all your homework, which is what this book is about and what we will dig into as we go. What you can also do is become one with the camera and one with the stage. The more experience you have on the stage and on the screen, the more you will become used to these false environments and the more easily and freely you can transcend them to secure the best performance, which is your job.

In screen training, many teachers tell you to ignore the camera. That's fine, because the camera can be repositioned to catch your behavior. However the great actors have a *relationship* with the camera and a *relationship* with the stage and audience. To them, the film set and the theatre are as homely as their own living rooms. When they step out on the stage, they appear to belong there. The stage itself, as a living entity seems to come alive when they arrive. The camera seems to want to watch them. There seems to be a communication going on between the actor and the camera in the film process and between the actor, the stage and the entire theatre in the theatrical process.

Sometimes we call this "presence". What is that? And how do you get it? First of all by knowing the dynamics of the camera and theatre intimately, and secondly, by triangulation, that is including the camera or the audience in a three-way, ritual communication. You're not playing up to the camera or the audience. You're involving these things, including them, embracing them in the process. It is the opposite of ignoring them. The difference between a performance that is inclusive of the camera or the audience in that triangulation and one that is not inclusive of it is so vast it is immeasurable. It smashes the idea of ignoring the camera to pieces. Once you have felt that feeling of perfect triangulation, once you have seen it back on screen, you will wonder what the hell you were ever doing before. Suddenly you have these nebulous things that the industry bandy around and can't define, like x-factor or star-quality going on in your own performances. A performance without triangulation is akin to going to a lecture where the professor is reading into his beard, can't be heard, can't be seen and seems to have no passion for his subject and certainly no will to communicate his subject to his students. A performance with triangulation is quite the opposite. He doesn't look you in the eye necessarily, but he seems to be speaking to you as an individual even though there are sixty other people in the theatre. He seems larger than life, being driven by some primal force that has fired his connection to his subject and his subsequent passion for it. Ever seen acting like that? It's rare, but it happens; and you can do it too. There's no magic to it and it is no longer confined to some "elite" of gifted actors that you should feel ostracized from. However, you can't fake it either. You need to do your homework, apply triangulation to it, practice is over and over and with experience it comes. And when it comes you know it. It's a sensation like nothing else.

I just mentioned practice. The more you run scenes in front of a camera and on the stage using triangulation at the end of all your other homework, the better you get at it until it becomes second nature. Soon it actually becomes part of you and your process. You have it even in life. You walk into a room and you carry it there too. Your energy seems to be exuding from you, pulsing outward to those around you. Your introversion goes away and for many of my students I have seen that introversion and self-consciousness disappear forever.

Without working with the camera in this way, there is little point to camera classes. Sure you can shoot something, watch it back, make sure it is believable and not contrived, do it again, watch it back again and so on and so forth, and that is all good, but that's not camera or screen training. That's a basic acting class where you are using the camera to check if you are being "real" or not by recording your performance and watching it back. Sometimes a teacher might advise you that your performance is too "big" for the screen and encourage you to make it "smaller". Watch the way your performance loses all of its life and truth by following such a directive. Really if you want to step into the world of the big boys and girls as a screen actor, you should be taking natural and believable behavior as assumed and be moving on to fairly sophisticated ideas such as triangulation or at the very least similar concepts such as Chekhov's "radiation". In a good screen class you should be studying these kinds of methodologies in minute detail, in different sized shots and frames using different kinds of cameras and framing options.

So what is it that you are triangulating? What are you trying to exude, radiate or send out to the camera? In the second stage of triangulation we flip it slightly and ask, what are you trying to draw the camera or the audience towards? In our studio, this thing is called the "essence of the character". Again that title suggests something ethereal or vague, but it is quite the opposite. We all have an essence that is us. Call it your personality, your persona, your character, or something a little more religious like your soul or spirit, whatever way you want to word it you have an essence that is uniquely you; a presence that speaks of you that is different to any other person's essence on this planet. It identifies you to others in a way that is over and above your physical appearance. Look at a room full of people and try to think of them in these terms. Each person is different, yes. Let us say that each one has a unique essence. Let us then suggest that we can *create* the unique essence of our character also. Imagine then that a certain character from a film or play is also in that room, unique and individual. They have an essence that is just as palpable as anyone else there.

One of the most interesting acting lessons is that line-up scene in "The Usual Suspects". All these fine actors are standing in a line, in character, and the essence of each of those characters is vastly different to the one beside it. Of course we find out later that Kevin Spacey's character had invented another persona on top of the "real" persona of the character. His job is to invent an invented persona, which leads to the brilliant twist in the film. Each of those actors is building their character's essence using their own individual technique. For some it is very physical and vocal in terms of transformation. For others it is the creation of an individual attitude or mood using psychological detailing. For others they have decided to play it pretty much as themselves and assume the audience will accept them to be the character they say they are. They are all telling the story, but in different ways using their different approaches to their art. They have all found an individual essence of their character, which is why the film still works despite the vast range of acting styles on display.

It's that essence that we are sharing with the other character in the scene, and in this work of triangulation, sharing with the camera and the audience. If you think this way as an actor, it is your job to build that character in order to find its essence and hence tell the story of that unique human being. As you tell it then, using a simplistic analogy, you include the audience in it in the same way that you read a book to a child and keep the child engaged and glued to your storytelling as you go along. If you can do this, your mind, body and all your senses can be filled with the character's essence. As such there will be no room in you for your own self-consciousness, your own anxieties and your worries about your lines. Indeed all the distractions that can threaten to make your performance "bad" will go away completely, and the audience notices it.

I will reiterate a maxim that my students know me for and discuss it a bit. "Acting is about the character first, the other character in the scene second, the audience third and the actor comes in a distant fourth. Let's be a little clearer on what this proverb has become. First of all, numbers 1, 2 and 3 are all number 1. They are of equal importance. They are dealt with by the actor in rehearsal in that order, but in the act of performance they are all one.

Let's look at number 4, the actor. I don't want to give the impression that I think the actor is unimportant in the process. After all, nothing can happen without her. All of numbers 1, 2 and 3 are contingent on the actor having her act together. However from my long years of experience, it is the selfless actor that achieves the greatest results. I encourage generosity and selflessness in my actors and students at all times, both in their lives and in the studio and further, on the stage and on the set. Generous people's energies go out rather than in. Their presence is magnetic. They are looking outwardly, searching for the next thing they can do to help someone else. People gravitate to them. Deals are struck, plans are made and great things are achieved. It is a joy to work with such a person.

On the other hand, there are many actors out there who are deeply selfish. They are thinking of everyone around them as a stepping-stone to their own success. The process of working with such a person becomes an intricate battle of wills and diplomacy. It is the worst way to work and the results on the stage are evident. Numbers 1, 2 and 3 in that maxim are being manipulated to the ends of the actor. "I'll create this character to show off this or that side of my talent. That actor seems to be getting more attention than me, so I'll draw that attention to myself and isolate them on the stage. This audience is my paycheque. This whole production is a tool for me to promote myself. As such I'll show off as much as I can. I don't care about the story or the character." Even before an actor has outwardly demonstrated this selfishness, after a time of working in theatre, you can smell it, and it always reveals itself eventually.

Stanislavski tried to convince his actors to live their lives in the same way they approach their work. It's simply a matter of practice. Change your thinking so that your energies are going towards elevating someone else (the character, the other actor, the audience, the production as a whole) rather than yourself. In our business, it is so damn hard to get work that if you try to spend all your time promoting yourself, with the precious little results it will achieve, it will certainly leave you bitter and twisted. You should not feel jealous when someone gets a great role and you haven't worked for six months. What a crappy way is that to live? And when you do get a great role, you should not think of yourself as rising above all around you, pretending you never knew those people who gave you so much in your past struggles, you should try in every way you can to bring them along with your success. Perhaps you believe in karma or whatever, but more than likely your generosity will reap its rewards in time. But even if you don't believe in karma, and even if you keep on giving and keep on getting slapped and getting nothing back, you will feel an awful lot better than the bitter and twisted actor exploiting the resources of all around him.

And better than that again, and here's the important point, your work on the stage or screen will be a thousand times better. In audition technique classes, I insist that bitterness, ego, nervousness and desperation can be picked up by a camera, no matter how hard you try to bury them down. If you *actually* feel great because a friend got a great part last week, if you *actually* don't mind if someone else gets the part you are auditioning for if the director thinks they are better suited, if you *actually* have creatively done your homework on the part and created an interesting, artistic interpretation for the role rather than your homework consisting of, "how can I get an advantage over everyone else auditioning", you will walk into that room beaming that truly positive presence into the place. You will have *real* confidence. Not the fake confidence of "I'll put on my cheesy smile, compliment everyone, get my cleavage out and flirt", which always makes anyone with any dignity feel icky afterwards. Trust me that directors, producers, agents and casting agents can smell your desperation a mile away. Do you really think you are the first actress to flash them a wink or a lingering look? (Vice versa here of course gender-wise.) Do you really think they haven't seen the James Dean to-cool-for-school act before? What they are looking for is someone they can have an honest conversation with. They want to find someone they can work with, negotiate with and communicate with. They want someone who has the talent, training and knowledge to make the project work and have a great day on set or in the rehearsal studio at the same time. If they can find that there is also the chance of a long-standing collaboration developing and maybe a few beers afterwards too.

Scorcese didn't make all those films with De Niro because they couldn't communicate. They made them because they could and because it was a joy. I'm sure they too had their battles from time to time, but there is no way that the work they created could have become what it is without a relationship of communication and common vision.

It's hard to make it a part of actual training, but it is true that the way you live your life while tipping along in this very difficult business brings greater capacity for excellence in your work and a much greater chance of you nailing those auditions and booking those gigs. It's bloody hard to remain positive in an industry that is often closed off, cliquey and monopolized by uncreative people making bad decisions. It's very hard to watch someone balls up a great movie or play when you know that a couple of different decisions could have avoided it. It's tough to watch bad movies get funded and made when excellent, risky scripts can't get a look in. It's hard then to see the critics and public praise what you know is mediocre work, knowing it could have been so much better. But that's life and I'd imagine it's the same in any business or corporate environment. You need to accept that and live your own life in the art free of these awful negative feelings.

If I may tell a brief story that easily emphasizes this, I was recently working on the TV series, The Vikings. I had a small role, about sixteen lines in the final episode of the first series. I'm sure he won't mind me saying so, on the set, the lead actor, Travis Fimmel was creatively orchestrating his character's arc throughout the five days I was with him on set. He had a huge responsibility to help make a thirty million Euro project enormously successful. I was picked up first by the driver during those five days of shooting. We then went to Trav's place to pick him up, the light just touching the horizon. Down he comes from his apartment with three cups of coffee made from his own coffee machine, one for the driver, one for himself and one for me. We chatted about our common home country, Australia throughout those days. He was relaxed, assured and professional, yet rarely overly serious. He never once talked about acting or his process. He joked with the other actors. Things were kept light and the piss was healthily taken. Then when the shot was being set up, sometimes right in the middle of a conversation, Trav would simply walk away into the forest, collect his thoughts and wander back. He would look at the way the shot was set and ask the director to focus at certain moments on me and the other minor roles. He was active in the direction and communicated with the director constantly. He pushed me forward in front of him rather than behind him. Everyone on set loved his company, his wicked sense of humor and his generosity. At one point we even had a light-hearted argument about who should stand where. "Come on, you go in front." "You're the lead, mate. Get your arse up there." Can you even imagine a better way to work? Look at the series. It's evident, even on the screen. Some fantastic scenes between us were cut from that final episode and I barely feature at all. I could get down and bitter about that. I can resent it. I can get depressed and wonder if I gave a shit performance, but the truth is I don't mind one bit. The editors used what they needed to tell the story. They shot far too much material and introduced a new character very late in the series. Mine. Trav and me and the others did our jobs well. Although I will never see those scenes, I know they were good. They had more great material than they could possibly use and that's just how the cookie crumbled. It's not about me. It's about the best way of telling the story. Besides that, because I was so lightly featured it leaves open the possibility of getting another, possibly larger role on it down the track. Happy days.

Allow me momentarily to dwell on this whole industry game in a slightly more personal way. Since we were kids we have been categorized. You were either a "sporty type" or an "academic type" or an "arty type". Kids then tribalize themselves and parents and teachers expect and assume certain behaviors. If you break out of those behaviors it confuses people. A sporty type can't be arty. An arty type can't be sporty and the academic types will always get better grades than the other two types.

I don't think my experience has been very different to everyone else's and people tried to pigeon hole me as an actor from a very early age. Ok, he can act, but what actor is he? Is he "the next" James Dean? Is he "the next" Marlon Brando. Is he "the next" Gregory Peck. As soon as that thinking starts, the focus on the art of acting is gone. One director I had at University thought I would be a great romantic lead and so I played several of those. When I got into acting school I was no longer among the good-looking guys. Veritable fashion models had been brought into that group. "Oh we need to give the romantic and heroic leads to the good-looking guys. David can play bit parts of quirky characters." Then out into the industry and my first agent was a very attractive gay man who spent a great deal of time with very attractive gay men and of course I was really the antithesis of that so he sent me for auditions for the roles of geeks, freaks and outcasts. The fact is I can play any one of those parts from romantic leads to freaks and geeks and have, however the agents and industry people have no way of being able to accept that. They must pigeon hole you. They will try to fit you into a type in their books. Here are my "James Dean" types. "Here are my Winona Ryder types". (Just as a quick aside, that University director did once offer me a choice of parts in a play; the heroic lead or his elderly mother. Fair play to her. I chose the mother.)

The fact is industry people instinctively pigeon hole you by what they see and perceive in front of them and what they see currently on the TV and stage and in magazines. As such the whole process of evolution of the art is painfully slow because the people who are running the professional side of it are constantly maintaining the status quo by regurgitating its types. The actual person they see must be the kind of character you can play and nothing else, which of course means that you have to decide which one of those actor "types" you are going to be and then play that out in your day to day life to such a degree that it becomes embodied more or less. You then have to pray that you are convincing in that type and will get work playing a very small subset of characters. It is a stupid exercise that never works. Yes, Luke Perry is the James Dean type. But we can all see the attempted imitation and it grates. It is also an exercise in completely ignoring who you are as a person. It is an exercise in falseness and pretense in which I was never interested. I may live to regret not playing that game, but I did not want to buff up to be the romantic lead. I liked being mercurial physically so that in one play I could play a burly soldier and the very next a frail eighty-year old man or a pantomime dame. And you know what? Brando, Dean and Peck could do all that too and so rarely got the chance.

I recall at acting school being introduced to this hocus pocus thing called an Enneagram. Well, to be fair it may not be hocus pocus, but it was certainly presented as hocus pocus to me, twisted to attempt to make it relevant to acting. I can't even remember the details of it, but it essentially was a circular diagram that led you to being able to decide which one of about nine human "types" you were. It was decided that I was the "Devil's Advocate". Another type was the "Tragic Artist" and there were several others. I remember the teacher saying to me, "there! Now you know! That's your personality. Devil's Advocate characters are the ones you should focus on in your career!"

Through unkind thoughts of suddenly snapping her neck like a chicken, I said, "but I don't think this is accurate. There's no science here to start with... and besides that I don't think I am a Devil's Advocate. I might be sometimes in life, but certainly not in others. Besides, surely the actor's job is to be flexible enough to transform and play many different characters. I'm nineteen years old. I don't know who I am."

Although I can't remember the details of the diagram, I will never forget what was said next. She said, "well you have to know your type to be an actor." She then walked away and reported my "resistance" to the head of school who brought me to task over it.

I looked at that diagram again and I remember thinking that there were two people I knew who definitely did not fit into one of those categories. Me and Hamlet. Here is a man who has lost his father, as has Laertes, as has Ophelia, as has Fortinbras and he watches or at least learns of Laertes' anger, Ophelia's suicide and the nobility of Fortinbras, but he still does not know how to behave. He is not the Laertes type, or the Ophelia type or the Fortinbras type and trying to be one of them instead of being himself and waiting for his own spirit to take action is what this play is all about and why (I think) it is so long. Shakespeare has to let it unfold naturally. It was the first great experiment in writing a character that could not be defined by type. That process takes time. And then eventually the moment of the dual with Laertes arrives and Hamlet knows that this moment will reveal his true essence. And he says to his so patient friend Horatio who appeals to him not to fight the dual, "The readiness is all." "Let be."

If Hamlet doesn't fit into the Enneagram, how can anyone play him?

So let me remind us both why I am going on like this. Let be. The fine actor is an actor who can play any character, whatever anyone in the industry tells you otherwise. The actor can be distracted by a lack of homework, lack of confidence in his or her ability, envy and jealousy of others, desperation, confusion and pressure in a tough game, lack of self-esteem about her looks, lack of technique, fear of the camera or the audience, depression about the mediocrity created by those in power, and probably a whole truckload of other baggage that I haven't mentioned. For Christ's sake, people! How do you expect to act well with all that bouncing around in your freaked out noggin? Worse again, how do you expect to have your body, your mind and your palate of your sensations available to a character when your own feelings are a mix of nerves, uncertainty and petty hatreds? You need to find yourself a way of working that brings you to true peace with yourself and your work and casts all these unhelpful distractions into the bottom of the deep. Once you can do that there are real possibilities of immersion and immersive acting. There is the possibility of someone else called the character actually living through you without you worrying about it, manipulating and getting in its way. You need to find a way that works.

So let's do just that.

The Possible Someone

THE CULT OF "NO CHARACTER"

In recent years a movement of "NO CHARACTER" has invaded the thinking of actors and actor training, especially audition technique training. This movement has been driven by exasperation and is the result of long years of trial and error and development that has led, in the eyes of some, to nothing much.

Stanislavski started his work with the classic thesis of "What if this was me in this situation? What would I do? How would I react? How would I behave?" Of course, quite quickly after that his student Michael Chekhov thought it best not to put such weight on the actor him or herself and instead to ask another question, "What would the character do in this situation? How would he or she react, behave etc." Another student of Stanislavski, Meyerhold looked at other approaches altogether, mostly to do with the body as a mechanism for narrative. Coming around a one hundred year circle, many teachers, particularly those caught up in the "business" of casting film and television would prefer actors to neglect any idea of character and trust the fact that if they have been called to audition for a particular role, more than likely they have been invited according to their type, not their ability to build a character. They already *are* the character: the same age, the same height, the same weight, the same nationality and the same background. Now all they have to do is say the lines, sound natural and look pretty to their pre-prophesized audience. These teachers have reverted right back to "what if this was me in this situation. I'll do this as me." Or perhaps they never left that place. The "talent" in this kind of approach to acting is in the skill of being totally natural and giving to the camera what the audience might want to see. As such there is no character. There's the actor bringing her own personality to the work and filtering everything through that.

In a way I have no problem with this system. I can't because I have to be honest with myself that I am training actors to get jobs and make a living to some degree. So yes, you need to know how to hit the right note with the director and the casting people and as such the audience. But this is the "X-factor" of the acting world. It is artless and to me mediocre and boring. It is easy to train actors to do this. What's more interesting, more challenging and more inspiring is the idea of living a life that is not yours and doing it through a whole other parameter of expression.

All art, to some extent, carries the stamp of the artist. There's no getting away from that and nor should we want to or need to. However there is a place in art that belongs to the subject and the subject in acting is the character in the same way that the subject in painting is the bowl of fruit and in music is the piece. Constantine, Hamlet, Ophelia and Blanch are artistic subjects. They require more than a stroking of the actor's ego to make them come alive.

At the end of the day we are telling a story to an audience. What does the audience think when viewing the art? They think about the subject, the character. They might occasionally think of the artist's process in building it, but if we have done our job right, only after the event. When you go to see a Bacon exhibition, yes, you know that it's Bacon, but Bacon knows he has done his job right when you forget about him for a while at least while viewing his work and allow the pictures to sweep you away into a sensory place of thinking, narrative and action. Afterwards we can sip coffee and be in awe of the brilliance of Bacon, but Bacon doesn't want or need that. Bacon is offering you a subject to consider.

If the actor does nothing more than stroke his or her own need to be loved by the audience, there is little point in being anything more than a professional celebrity. And if a cult of this kind of approach to acting takes precedence in the world of acting as an art form, acting itself cannot and will not evolve in the way that all art should and must. A vast period of stagnation will become entrenched, and all characters and all storytelling must wait until it grows tiresome and passes.

The Possible Someone

FOUR STATEMENTS

Let's broach and consider four statements about acting and the actor's relationship with the audience before moving on. It's good to keep these in mind.

1. If I understand the text, the audience will understand it.

2. If the text is special to me, it will be special to the audience.

3. If I am moved emotionally, my audience will be moved emotionally.

4. If I tell the story effectively, the audience will follow it and go with me.

The only ones of these that stand up in any kind of complete way are the first one and the last one, and they are obviously connected. I really should understand what I'm saying and what this story is about. If I don't, I can't expect the audience to understand it and I shouldn't be surprised if the audience disconnects and goes home at the interval.

If you tell a story to a child, they follow along with it because you understand the story thoroughly and you are telling it in the right way. You are connecting with them, sharing images with them, speaking clearly so they can hear you fully, moving through it at a good and true pace that is not too fast so that the child cannot digest the images and words and not too slow so that the child gets bored.

So what's the difference between telling a children's story and acting to an audience. The essential difference of course is that you are not narrating what's happening, but revealing the story through the character itself. You are not a "storyteller" but a "character". You can't suddenly turn to the audience or the camera and say, "Oh, by the way, in case you didn't get it, the wolf is up on the top of the house." (Unless it's a soliloquy of course which is rare in film.) All you can do is be the piggy in the brick house, with his two terrified brothers with him who have just had their houses destroyed by the wolf, listening to the wolf getting up on the roof and getting ready to slide down the chimney. You have an idea! Light a fire and stick a big pot of boiling water on it! That'll screw him!

Your actions tell the story. You can't narrate it.

Now, as an actor, you might just love this story and the piggy's words and think that you can convey to the audience just how special you think this story is by indulging in certain moments and drawing them out, perhaps emphasizing certain bits of text that you think are wonderful and sort of subconsciously showing the audience how special this text is to you. However as soon as you try to do this, you're not telling the story anymore. There's another kind of distracting dynamic going on. Sure, the audience might think it's a special story too, but just because you do doesn't mean they will and you can't force them to.

Similarly, you as an actor may be filled with wonderful emotions and sensations in this moment; fear, determination and powerful feelings of protectiveness of your brothers may be filling you. You are being moved by your immersion as this piggy in the given circumstances. That's great and may well inform your behavior, the quality of your gestures and movement and totally support the telling of the story. However you can't expect the audience to feel that fear, for example, just because you're feeling it. It's kind of akin to saying, "look audience! Look how scared I'm feeling and how that's informing my behavior. Don't you feel really really scared too? Oh, you don't? Well I better act a whole lot more scared to try to make you feel the fear I think you should be feeling. Perhaps I should cry a bit." The audience isn't scared because you are acting scared. They are scared because there's a wolf on the roof and they don't know what they would do in the same situation. They are dying to know what you'll do to solve it, so that they can do the same if they're ever in the same situation.

You can't force them to feel something. It won't work because your attempts to infect your audience with an emotion immediately stop those emotions from being genuinely felt by that little piggy you are playing. Now those emotions are tools that you are trying to use to manipulate the feelings of the audience. It will come across as contrived. If you live it, triangulate it by being aware that it is being read, the audience will feel whatever they are meant to feel in that moment. Some will be afraid, some will be exhilarated by the moment and some will not care because this story doesn't turn them on. That's not up to you.

Understand it and tell the story well. Being connected in a special way with the text and the character will help and so will being accessible to sensations on behalf of the character. But trying to sell those things to the audience will not work.

Let's keep this in mind especially when we talk about triangulation. It can so easily be misconstrued as an attempt to force the audience to feel a certain way or see a certain thing you are trying to do. That's not it. It's an awareness that you are being watched and read and that this thing we do is a ritual communication between actors and audience where the essence of the character is being revealed.

To conclude, let's keep a compass. True north is that which tells the story well. Anything that doesn't follow this trajectory is of little use to us.

The Possible Someone

WHAT EXACTLY IS CHARACTERISATION?

We've already covered this in a roundabout way, however I'd like to nail this down in fairly simple language once and for all.

This is the big problem, right here. How does one go about the process of characterization if one doesn't even know what characterization means and indeed what it is? I was very good at mathematics in my early teens, but when it came time to deal with the big tricky stuff later on, like trigonometry and calculus, I hit a wall. Frankly, I just couldn't do it. No teacher was able to teach it to me. I was called stupid. It wasn't until years later that I realized I couldn't solve those advanced types of mathematical equations because I didn't know what trigonometry and calculus were. What was the motivation behind them? What was the purpose of them? Why were they invented and who invented them? What did they actually *mean*?

Of course this is a blasting indictment on the teachers who mis-taught me those things. So lets not mis-teach things, shall we? Instead lets know what characterization is, what its purpose is, where it comes from and what we can hope to achieve by it. Let's do this firstly as simplistically as possible and then look at the complexities of the process.

Characterization is the act of creating a character rather than playing yourself. That's a simple enough idea. It's been around for about two hundred years as a term, although Thespis himself was arguably creating characters rather than playing himself a couple of thousand years ago. Many teachers including Stanislavski and Chekhov thought long and hard about it. It's a simple statement but it's much more complex when you start to ask questions like, "Where does the actor and character separate?" "What should happen to me when I get into character?" "How do I know I'm in character?"

The purpose behind characterization is to do with the audience. We are hoping that the audience will be watching the character on stage or screen, not an actor saying lines. We hope it will absorb them into the story and help them to suspend their disbelief very early on. We want to use this thing called characterization to help us tell the story in an effective way. Some will argue that, in our times when the Hollywood star system is prevalent, the audience is coming to see the actor anyway. The character is irrelevant. The audience is going to see Tom Cruise, so what's the point of Tom Cruise turning himself into anything other than Tom Cruise? Strangely, however, the Academy still rewards characterization and especially transformative characterization at its big, flashy award ceremony where all these actors flaunt themselves in front of millions of people. It's an odd little contradiction, but a fascinating one.

So what is a character? A character is a human being in a drama with a crisis going on and something they desperately want to achieve. As an actor you can understand that crisis, feel a sense of ownership of it, learn the lines and do it as you. It is arguable that you are already playing a character, because the crisis isn't yours. It's someone else's and you are taking it on, reacting according to it, saying words that are not your own, but that belong to the character and playing out a series of actions that you might not play out if you found yourself in the same situation. As such, if you are taking on someone else's crisis, saying their words and playing out their actions, it stands to reason that you might start to feel like you're someone else. You might sense that you are thinking someone else's thoughts and feeling someone else's feelings and behaving differently.

Now it's here that some quarters of thinking will criticize what's happening to you, accusing you of being indulgent, suggesting that no one cares what you're feeling or that your feelings are irrelevant. However, anything and everything that's happening to you while you are acting is interesting and important both externally and internally, especially to me as your teacher. What are you going to do? Not feel? It's rather like telling a fish to get out of the sea.

The question now arises, how much do I need to do to *become* this person more fully? That's up to you and your production. It also depends on the nature of the character. If you're playing an historical figure or a person with a peculiar physicality or psychology, you'll sense that there are certain differences or separations between the person that is you and the person that is the character. You may feel the need, if you truly want their story to be told in the "right" way, to transform yourself into a convincing guise that speaks of them rather than you and hence bridge those separations. That is the process of transformational characterization, and the more you transform the more you will begin to feel like you are someone else rather than yourself. You are literally lending your entire faculty, mind, body and senses, to this other life. You will begin to create someone "new". A "possible someone" that you and your director might like to present to the audience and have the story told through that "possible someone" rather than yourself. In turn, the more you transform, the more you will feel that you are convincingly the character. You will feel "immersed" in them, rather than in yourself.

Now, here's an interesting extension of these ideas. In life you meet people you are drawn to and people who repel you. Sometimes you are very drawn to someone and sometimes very repulsed by someone else. Usually you sit somewhere in the middle of these two poles with most people you meet. Sometimes you meet someone that you want to spend lots of time with and get to know. They seem to fascinate you on some level. That could be a romantic level or a business level or in some way that you can't really nail down. You just know you like them. You're curious about what makes them tick and the person they are. Think about those people in your life and try to isolate exactly what it is that draws you to them. It could be a number of things: their looks, their intellect, their disposition, their courage, their shyness, their sense of humor, their talent, or their history. Now ask yourself, if you were an audience member, how might I be drawn to this character you are working on playing? How is my audience going to be fascinated by this character I'm going to be playing? What's going to draw them to me and make them want to know more about me and follow my story? Conversely, think about those people you don't like and don't want to spend time with. Are they rude, self-absorbed, cruel or manipulative? If you are playing a villain, you might want your audience to hate you, but you need to find that level to the character that makes the audience love to hate them. Take Heath's Joker or Hannibal Lector as examples. What is it about them that make them fascinating too? As such, the work that Heath Ledger has to do as the Joker is going to be different to the work Christian Bale will be doing as Batman. Christian is working out the dual substance of Bruce Wayne. Heath is building a psychopath who "just wants to watch the world burn". When the director combines the work of both actors, the enormity of the conflict emerges and if everything is done right, the audience is equally fascinated by both characters and the intricate battle between them.

You may be nothing like the character you are going to be playing. You may not have their infectious charm or sense of humor, or indeed their cruelty or manipulative nature. Similarly you may not have the physical shape or build or idiosyncratic pattern that your research and imagination are suggesting. In the work of characterization, you don't need to have those things as part of the person that is you. You find them through the character. You find *their* charm or *their* sense of humor during the process of working *through* them. You find their physical life too. Usually this requires your imagination and a sharp intellect on your part. It also requires an adaptable body.

THE LONELY PROTAGONIST

If you are asked to play a lead role there is another level of thinking that needs to come into play in your work.

The protagonist of a play is lonely, and this loneliness can often make the character inaccessible to the audience if the actor's work hasn't been done right. He or she is the character to whom the audience relates most closely and this relationship manifests itself on several levels. Firstly, the protagonist is suffering a certain level of solitude in its efforts to solve the Core Problem. Other characters may assist them, but at the end of the day they will have to do it themselves. They often die at the end, and dying is something all of us must do alone. Macbeth, Hamlet, Walter White and Blanch are immersed in a particular loneliness within themselves. In order to bring the audience along with them in their journey, the actor must subtly reveal the nature of that loneliness so that the audience can enter their world. They must be brought on a journey with the character, understand his or her thinking and consider their problem almost as their own. Often these Core Problems are deeply human and poetic and of great interest to a thinking audience. Occasionally, especially in theatre there may be more than one character that the audience relates to on this kind of level. In film, the general rule of script writing is to ask, "whose story is it?" and we follow that one through-line throughout. However those simplistic rules are generally designed to make the film appealing to a mass audience rather than a thinking, niche audience.

There's a huge responsibility here, as you can imagine, but in essence the work is no different to the work one does in developing any character of any size. It's fair to say however, that the intensity of the triangulation, the connection with the camera and the audience is vitally important when playing the lonely protagonist.

Further to this, lead characters are complex animals in that they often don't know exactly what their Objectives are. Hamlet doesn't quite know what to do about the fact that he suspects his father has been murdered. Marlene doesn't know exactly why she has gravitated back to Joyce and Angie in Top Girls. Alison in Look Back in Anger doesn't know why she has returned to her and Jimmy's old haunt, where Helena has taken her place in Jimmy's bed. These are mighty characters and they reflect an extra layer to the truths of our humanity, that we ourselves often don't know what we want, we don't know what our purpose is and we certainly don't know why we exist, even if we have certain beliefs about those things. Therefore the theory that every character has a simple, single Objective collapses when you have to look at the more complex characters of dramatic literature.

As such then, we cannot only act for our own satisfaction. We must take the audience into account and ensure they are being accessed and told the story. As much as we desire that feeling of total immersion, there is no point to it at all if the audience are sitting outside the thing, disconnected from all your wonderful, immersive acting. Simplistically speaking, just because you're "in it" doesn't mean they are. And they must be.

So once again we are able to clarify some mysterious terminology of the industry or the business. When you hear someone say, or a reviewer write, "her character was unsympathetic" or "he played an unsympathetic character well" or "I didn't care about the character", what they mean is that they personally did not sympathize with the character. If that's the case the actor did not draw the audience into the character's sadness and loneliness. That could be a choice or a mistake. The complex character on the page is never sympathetic or unsympathetic. If depends entirely on how the actor chooses to play him and what the director is trying to achieve overall.

When you hear someone referred to as a leading actor, or even an A-list actor, these are the actors who have been proven to most effectively bring their audience on the journey of their characters while playing leading roles. They do that in different ways and for different audiences, but they can command an audience and many people want to come and see them. Orlando Bloom absorbs his female fan base for the most part because of his looks. Brendan Gleeson, Liam Neeson, Cate Blanchet and others are drawing their audience in through their own approaches to characterization and their story-telling ability as actors, and each of those approaches is different and individual. Johnny Depp is damn good looking, and not as bad story-telling actor too. At some point they were lucky enough to get that thing called a "break" and proved they could do this in a leading role. Then they were bankable and were asked to do it again and again. They will keep on being asked as long as the audience continues to respond to them and be drawn into the stories of their characters. If a bad choice of project causes the audience to react irksomely to a movie or a play, they might slip off that A-List. As such, once you're up there, the pressure is very much on to stay there if you want to play the Hollywood game. In turn, many actors choose to behave badly in public so they will end up splashed all over tabloid newspapers. This keeps them in the news and their profile high. Then, when they are about to appear in a new movie, the audience recognizes them immediately and their curiosity is aroused enough to get them into the cinema. So yes, the tabloids are often attacked for being overly aggressive, but many "stars" want their attention equally as aggressively and plan their entire tabloid persona to a tee.

Anyway, let's not worry too much about the trappings of the industry. You will never entirely disappear when you act, even if you feel that you have. You, in the process, are very important because you are the artist creating the work of art. You are doing that for your audience, your ensemble and your character.

Most importantly, however, you need to be available for the character despite the parameters of your own personality. If you want to tell the story of your character, if you want to draw the audience into the character's loneliness and thinking rather than into your own, you need to get out of its way and think about what you need to do to "become" them, not for the sake of changing from yourself into the character, but for the sake of the story and the audience watching it.

YOU IN THE PROCESS

In my fulltime training process I give each of my student actors a length of dowel about four to five feet long. I ask them to balance this thin stick on its end on the middle finger of their favored hand. This is not a new exercise. It has been used by dance and physical theatre trainers from Meyerhold and onwards. It sounds like a simple enough exercise in balance and for some it is. For others it isn't. Immediately knowing it is a simple exercise, the actor becomes frustrated when the stick teeters or falls completely. They become embarrassed. They start to look around them and see that a few of the others are doing it. "Why can't I? I'm shit. I can't even balance a stick on my finger." So they then pick the stick up and try it again doing *exactly the same thing*! They make no adjustment. They don't stop and ask why is this not working on a purely technical level. "Am I off balance? Am I not breathing calmly? Am I setting my eyes too high or too low on the stick when I try to balance it?" They just do it again making no changes because it's so damned important to them that the other actors don't get one up on them by balancing the stick better.

It's a great exercise to do early in the course because I can glean a real sense of the personality of each of the actors and the way they approach a challenge. I can see the one who thought she would grace her way through the course. I can see the cynical one who is wondering what he is paying fees for to stand around trying to balance a stick on his finger. I can see the ones that give up easily and the tenacious ones who attack the exercise a little too vehemently. I can see the ones who need work on their physicality and the ones who need to learn to breathe again. I can see the ones who are self-conscious that they are being watched and might make a watched mistake. And I can also see the one that drops the stick, picks it up, takes a second to consider why it was dropped, and without emotion makes an adjustment to his process and tries again. Soon he is balancing the stick adeptly, easily, calmly and in fact has achieved a true sense of grace in the exercise.

Without fail it is the ones who calmly adjust their own approach to the stick exercise who will absorb the technical training without fuss, without resistance and achieve extraordinary results in a short space of time. So my job then is to try to change the thinking of every actor in that group who is not that calm achiever. It's not about molding personalities or trying to change them as people. It's about finding a *way to work* that works. In that headspace creativity has a greater possibility of happening.

I won't go into details about how I go about making that creative space happen, but suffice to say it is about burning off a lot of self consciousness, self concern, jealousy that you might not be the best actor in the room and learning patience. Once you've got it, you'll never want to go back to that desperate way of moving through the stick exercise again. In fact you'll start to approach all your daily problems and your life itself in an entirely different way. And people sense it and they are drawn to you. In the studio you become an achiever. You begin to take real steps to wherever it is we are going. Most importantly, that way of operating bleeds into your approach to building characters. Instead of doing nothing and giving up, you start doing some research. You start to analyze the text and ask yourself creative questions. Soon you are becoming a thinking, creative actor, and that's the beginning of forming your own personalized technique.

For me as a teacher I have already been thinking about each actor individually before the course has started. After the stick exercise I make a lot of notes and I am right in the guts of diagnostic teaching.

Think of your scene and your role in the same way for a moment. You need to have a clear and creative headspace to let that character in, to accept the circumstances, to find true Objectives and begin your approach. If you are jealous that someone else is doing it better, fraught with tension physically or mentally or throwing up blockages in any other way, you are going to struggle. When it's not going right take a moment, think about your technical approach to it and ask useful questions about why it isn't happening for you. Then make a few adjustments that may be very simple and try it again.

In Charlie Rose's interview with Daniel Day-Lewis about There Will Be Blood, Daniel talks about the way he rarely watches the rushes during the filming. But at a certain point early in the shoot Anderson asks him to do just that. He agrees. He changes his own approach to the work at the behest of his director and together they see there is a problem. He makes some adjustments and then goes back to work. With all the bullshit one hears about Daniel being difficult to work with, that sounds to me like someone making sure the work is going in the right direction for the character, his director, the story and his audience rather than bullying on to please himself. He thought he was balancing the stick with grace when in fact it was wavering badly.

Once you have expelled the distractions that are to do with the needs of your own ego your attention goes onto those other three pillars, the character, the other character in the scene and your audience. Are they being told this story? Is the essence of the character being truly revealed?

Let's look at the other distractions we are talking about and look for some ways to work right in order to let them go.

Ask yourself, "What's going on in my head when I act?"

If you wish to be truly in character and truly immersed in it's world, surely your mind, sensations and body should be filled with stuff that is to do with your character and its world rather than filled with your stuff and your world.

Physically you need to be ready. Anything that physically pulls on you that is not to do with your character is going to end up being a distraction. Being tired, hung over, unfit or lethargic may not be the right place to be in for your character. You need to create a physical life for your character that makes you *feel* like you are behaving at least on their behalf and preferably *as* them. Actors do this in many different ways. We already talked about Hoffman's Marathon Man instance in which he created what he felt was the required exhaustion. Day-Lewis famously stayed in the physical shape of Christy Brown for My Left Foot for a long time both on and off set to make it convincing for himself and his audience. After all, all of Christy's behavior has to be filtered through that very unique physical pattern. How much work is too much work? There is surely never enough. Any moment caught on camera in which that physical life shows a fault or flaw is going to be useless to the editor. And what if a moment of falseness in that physicality should somehow make it into the movie? Awful!

These are perhaps extreme examples, but the work of Idiosyncratic Transformation, although difficult, at the very least gives you a sensation of being in another physical frame other than your own, and because the physical, the psychological and the emotional are so intimately connected in life, that physicality can and will inform sensations and thought processes that will not be your own but will be to do with the character. They will feel odd at first, these thoughts and feelings that don't belong to you, but once you let go of the need to control them they will build upon themselves as you develop the character and the project as a whole.

However even without Idiosyncratic Transformation, many actors do seemingly minor physical things to help them feel truly a part of the world of their character. Going back to The Vikings, I hadn't ridden a horse for a very long time. The character I was playing was a guide. He virtually lived on his horse and I wanted to feel that subconscious connection with the horse too. So I got a couple of lessons leading up to the shoot and went up a mountain or two. On set I stayed on the horse as much as I could and on the first day went off on a little jaunt through the forest on my own so that the horse and I could become acquainted and connected. I noticed Travis on several occasions dip his hands into the earth and smear real soil on his hands and costume in order to give him that extra sense of earthy reality that make-up dirt can't. Minor things yes, but again they bring the actor closer to the reality of the character's world. As such they help to rid the mind and body of the inevitable falseness of me being an actor pretending to be a king's guide in front of a big old camera, and make me more feasibly a king's guide. As such the camera picks up that reality rather than unfortunate moments of falseness. It picks up the essence of the character rather than an actor stumbling through an attempt to be convincing. I don't want to feel unconvincing to myself or to my audience. I think we both deserve better.

We are human beings, not robots. We have our troubles in life, our problems and our fears. We carry them around with us and try not to let them get the better of us. However in the audition technique work I teach, I notice that an actor's personal baggage is strangely picked up by the camera even when they are performing. You can see this kind of actor-nature coming through. It could be a bit of self-consciousness, or even some anger about a fight they've had with a boyfriend or something the night before. How do you solve that? It's easy to say, "Block all that out of your head!" but it's much more difficult to do. Our minds and sensations are always full of something. Achieving the nothingness of meditation is difficult and as actors can lead to a sense of void that isn't useful anyway. Instead it is better to fill the mind and sensations with the character's stuff. The character has a predicament, a core problem and at least one Objective. This character has images, memories and even sounds like music moving through her. In your homework you consider all that stuff and allow it to be understood intellectually, then allow that to drop into your body and the palate of your sensations. Fill yourself with that instead.

In The Art of Acting I wrote about Character Memory, Extended Imagery, Separations, Gesture, Tempo Rhythm, Character Traits and other tools that might help you to build the total mind and body of the character you are playing. Check in with those and ask yourself which ones appeal to you the most. Which one's help you to become absorbed in *being* the character fully? Which ones make you forget about yourself as an actor and make you feel like you are the character? For me it's the work of Idiosyncratic Transformation; that all absorbing shift in my physical self that leads me to feel like I'm actually looking at the world around me out of someone else's eyes. What is it for you? Is it the detailing of memories and images found in the text? Are you flooding your mind with the character's visions of memory and images and as such abandoning your own? And does that draw you into the world of the character's behavior? What is it that works for you?

So lets now put a few things together. You have a technique that takes you seamlessly through the basics. You have a technical pathway to advanced places and towards the essence of the character. You have a working, creative relationship with the stage and with the camera. You have an attitude and philosophy of selfless creativity. There should be no reason now why you are not making fine work. So let's get started on these advanced places.

INTERPRETING A ROLE

What is advanced acting then?

We know that in our modern, western stage, television and film work, we are required to achieve natural and convincing reality in most of it. As such then, let's assume that this is the most basic and fundamental achievement of the actor within the current, most popular styles. You can get this kind of training from a foundation course in acting at an institute, in a Stanislavski, Meisner, Adler or Strasberg fundamentals course or with any decent screen-acting tutor. Once you have the contrivances and woodenness knocked out of your acting, and as long as you can learn those lines well enough to make them not sound like they are being recited or read, you have achieved the naturalness of fundamental acting in the realms of *realism*. For some this takes a few weeks, for others a little longer especially if they have built up habits over years. Habits can be so engrained that removing them from the actor is often difficult. Many young actors who have spent their childhoods in stage schools will have habits of using demonstrative gestures and overly expressive emphasis on phrases and words. When you were a kid performing in your yearly stage show this was applauded by both your teachers and parents. In the reality of the grown-up world of acting, habits simply break the reality of the acting, causing it to come across as contrived and predetermined. The performance does not look like it is happening naturally in the moment. It looks like you have pre-decided to use a gesture or vocal emphasis on a certain line, because, well, you have. It is unconvincing and unnatural behavior.

Once you have solved these issues, can pursue an Objective in a concentrated way and allow your impulses to drive the action, you are ready for something a little more sophisticated. Let's look firstly at the way in which a role is interpreted.

At the outset, sure you get a script, read it, nut out what your character wants and the through-line of action that carries them to either achieving it or not and it looks reasonably convincing. But who is this person you are portraying? You can say those words and behave convincingly *as* you, through you. As we've discussed, many actors stop their work there and its very good and quite enjoyable. However, beneath that simple work is another entirely different world. We can call this *the character*. There is another way of wording the enquiry into character. "What *kind* of person is this?"

Poor writing usually ignores this and many of the "characters" seem to "sound" the same. The literary work of writing for the individual behavior and character traits of another human being is found in the more sophisticated writer's texts and it is in this realm of exploration that you as an actor can dig in and find out the *truth* about this human being you are portraying. So the first place to look for this extra dimensionality in the character is in the script itself. You start this process by asking the all-important question: Why?

Why is my character behaving like this?

Why is my character saying these exact words?

Let's say your character wants sex in a certain scene. It's definitely on the cards, though for some reason your character tip-toes around it even though they would be in like Flynn if they just went in for the kiss. That "some reason" is the clue to your character. It tells you about the *kind* of person you are dealing with.

Many new actors I train get handed a script by a great writer like Miller or Churchill and hand it back to me saying, "I don't get this character. I don't understand them and therefore cannot play them." What they very quickly discover, once I have handed the script right back to them, is that it is that very confusion that is the source of the river of their creativity. It is this confusion that will lead to an individual interpretation of the character. The thinking needs to be changed a little first of course. Instead of throwing your hands up in the air and declaring, "I can't do it!" the better approach is to say to yourself, "I don't get this character... yet. There is something curious and fascinating about this person and their behavior that I need to access." Therefore better "Why" questions, again, come to the fore. That scary "problem" you are sensing in the script is there because you *are not your character*. You would not behave the way they are behaving, you wouldn't say those words or talk that way, so your initial response is a kind of confusion because you cannot immediately relate to the character. "This doesn't make sense." "People don't do that." "People don't talk that way." Well your character is not "people". Your character is a unique individual and she *does* do what she does and she *does* say these words whether you like it or not. That's okay. Don't panic. Just ask a few questions.

Why do I not get this person?

Why is this person so different to me that I find their behavior impenetrable?

This person is *not* you. You are going to have to go and find them and come to an understanding of them in order to play them. That search *is* the work of the advanced actor. It is not a job without joy or a hard slog. It is a challenge and a great joy. All of the actor's technique, talent and creativity are going to now be awakened and come into play. This is the opportunity you have been waiting for.

Consider the great characters of dramatic literature. There are many of course, but lets list off a few we can play with. Oedipus, Hamlet, John Proctor, Willy Loman, Don Quixote. In the female department, Medea, Ophelia, Lady Macbeth, Blanch from Streetcar, Marlene and Joyce from Churchill's Top Girls, Nina from The Seagull, Alison from Look Back in Anger. What is it about these characters that makes them so interesting and considered "great"? Among other things, they penetrate something about the human condition that is common to all of us. They penetrated something that the audience of the time they were written responded to, and that response from audiences has continued. They have not aged. The first thing you need to do is find that one thing that makes this character so special. Imagine you were handed one of these roles. They are huge and complex in many ways and to look at them from the front might make you feel inferior or out of your depth. But the writers of these plays did not write them to make actors feel out of their depth. They wrote them with the earnest hope that there would be actors in the world who would make them come alive for the audience and bring them to the world.

It doesn't matter from whence you get that one thing. Hamlet has many fascinating facets, but to you it could be his grief for his father or his cynicism of the corrupt State, or even his sloth in taking meaningful action. Once you have found that one thing that makes the character so special to audiences, critics, academics, anybody, it makes no odds unless it has become something that is special to *you*. It must inspire you and charge you on to discover more and more about this incredible entity. You should begin to feel compelled to read everything you can about this person, who did what with it before, what they might have missed, and soon your imagination will burst into an artistic vision of what *you* are going to do with this person and once that happens, your technique comes into play. The brush is in hand, the canvas is on the easel and you are off and racing.

Something that is common among all those characters is that they all behave in very peculiar ways. When you read the script first you will wonder why. Once you have worked out why *for you*, everything will open up. That requires an imagination and yes it also requires an intellect. You need to do some thinking.

What *kind* of person is Hamlet? One actor will exclaim, "He is the great renaissance man!" Another, "He is a Prince!" Another, "He is a genius!" Another, "He is a coward!" Another, "He is a madman!" Another, namely me, "He is a reflection of the dual nature of man, confidence versus fear." What kind of person is Hamlet to *you*? What is the artist in you leaning towards? And if your idea has not been thought of before, don't be afraid of it. You are an artist. Remember? Those instincts may just be knocking on the door of something very, very important.

Now as an exercise, go and look up at least one of the characters I listed above and look for that thing that inspires you to learn more about them. In fact, do it with all of them! The truth of the matter is, if you can't find that which makes those characters fascinating, you may not be able to play them.

Let's get a little more detailed. Let's take an example of the character of Daniel Plainview in "There Will Be Blood". Here is a man who, on the outside, seems to have a single, simple Objective. Money. He seems to have no interest in women, family or religion. Damn! There's nothing to work with here! I'll just create a stereotype of a miser, make him a baddy and say the lines. However the better approach is to ask the question of "Why".

Why does Daniel have such a drive for wealth?

Why does he have no interest in family or women?

Why does he hate the church?

If you can answer these questions, you are well on the way to a much deeper interpretation of the character.

He is so interested in wealth because he is sick of poverty and thinks great wealth will make him happy.

He has had a bad experience with a woman in the past (whether its in the script or not) and has lost his faith in women and in the concept of love. Bigger and better again! Whatever has happened to him in the past has caused him to lose his faith in all people.

He hates the mass thinking of organized religion where everyone follows the teachings of the church like sheep. He has been alone for a long time and learned to think independently in order to survive. As such he feels he doesn't fit into the society around him.

Now go back to the script and see if anything in it supports these answers. At one point he says he just wants to make enough money to get away from people. Bingo. He is asked about his wife twice and both times avoids the subject, saying he doesn't want to talk about those things and in the other instance inventing a lie that she died in childbirth.

Now look hard and see what things in this script lead you to a deeper interpretation of Plainview as a miserly baddy? He adopts a child left by one of his dead workers. He doesn't know how to handle him, but he does. There's nowhere else for the child to go? Yes there is. He could take him to an orphanage somewhere. They did exist. Is he using the child as a pretty face to help his business? Arguable, yes and perhaps he is, but he also gets him the right kind of teachers when his hearing is damaged. He hugs him when he returns from boarding school. He connects with that child. His brother arrives and asks for work. He takes him on and makes him his right-hand man, only to find out the brother is a conman and not his brother at all. He does attempt in two small ways to have and hold real human relationships with other people that exist outside of his day-to-day work of searching for oil. He *wants* these things. Now we have a human being, not a cliché. Now we have someone who is not just malignant or malicious, but has a sadness and loneliness in him that could be like an enormous pool of molten lava under his heart. How far you choose to let that into the performance is up to you, and to some extent up to your director, but either way, you now have a character with another huge dimension to them other that the surface, money hungry, exploitative villain. You are on your way to the essence of the character.

There is more to find, much more, but this alone gives us a whole pallet to play with. On one hand we have a money hungry miser and on the other a deeply sad and lonely person. Character gold is in the sniffing! Why? In life we humans are full of contradictions. We have internal struggles going on all the time. We want two or three things often at the same time. We behave badly and behave wonderfully. We have dark and light sides to our natures. Once you have them both in a character you are finding complexity and human truth. I will write more soon about multiple Objectives and internal contradiction which will lead us more deeply into this idea.

So lets say now that we have this miser to play with. What misers do we know from history? Mr Burns from The Simpsons. Shylock from The Merchant of Venice. Moliere's Miser. All of these are based on the archetype of Pantalone from the Commedia Del Arte, a theatre tradition dating back hundreds of years. I know about Pantalone because I have *trained*. I have studied my art and know it well. I do some research and ask myself if I can create a twentieth century Pantalone drilling for oil in the Californian countryside? Why not? I look up the Pantalone mask, old etchings of Commedia performances, physical attributes such as the long fingers, the gangly frame, the hooked Jewish nose, the moustache. The moustache! Many men wore a moustache with no beard in the early and mid twentieth century. Brilliant. I look into the psychology of the Pantalone. He is exactly the miser in Plainview who would sell his daughter for the right price and uses her to attract wealthy suitors. This is all adding up. I do my physical work now. I start the process of Idiosyncratic Transformation, experimenting with his physicality. This takes time and patience, but results are beginning to show. Now lets knock on Stanislavski's door and seek the psychological and emotional inner life of Plainview and pit one against the other. You begin to see Plainview, feel him, play with nuances in his personality; how much of that inner pain he shows if any, how he performs for his audiences of villagers as he does deals and drills for more wealth. I get his accent right and find a tempo-rhythm and vocal quality that seems to suit. I live in his physical, vocal, psychological and emotional landscapes as much as I humanly can until he is embodied and I can behave as him subconsciously, moving through rooms, walking down hills, eating, drinking and washing. Now I have him and I'm ready for the camera.

Now I have no idea if that was Daniel Day-Lewis's process. I have never met the man so lets be clear that I'm not putting words in his mouth. As a teacher, however, I do look at the great performances and take a walk back through a possible creative approach that the actor may have taken to get the seemingly amazing result they have achieved. From the result however, one can take it as read that Day-Lewis has a masterful understanding of his craft and a watertight technique.

All right, so I hear you cry, "how often do you get given a script and character with that much depth to play with as "There Will Be Blood?" The answer is all the time and every time. It's just a matter of looking for it and finding it. I've rarely come across a script without its merits and without some depth to play with for the actor. Recently I played the role of a "villain" in seven episodes of a soap opera, and yes this dimensionality was even there too, hidden under the villain. Just because it's a soap opera doesn't mean the writing is complete rubbish. Much is worn on the sleeve, that's true. Often the editing makes you sigh or the quality of the shots bug you. Sometimes you would have liked more than one take. The audience are pretty much spoon-fed the story and if any criticism can be made of the script it is that there are often more words than is necessary. That said, even with this seemingly two-dimensional villain, there was a great depth of sadness and dissatisfaction in his seemingly perfect life that led him to behave so badly. That's the truth you need to find in your character. It is the truth in life too. When we behave badly it is usually to do with a very specific dissatisfaction in our own existence. Think of yourself as the character in the following scenarios and use Stanislavski's "I". I become jealous of someone. Why? Because I am insecure. I go out and get drunk and get in a fight. Why? Because I am dissatisfied with my life. I bully someone because I feel unhappy with myself and want them to feel unhappy too because it's unfair that they're happy and I'm not. I cheat on my partner because I am angry or lonely. I ruin my life by gambling away all my money because I have an addiction that controls me. You must get to the core of your character's dissatisfaction. That dissatisfaction will explain virtually all their behavior and why the play pans out the way it does. If you can do that, you can play the character truthfully and create an artistic interpretation of the character and the role.

This kind of thinking will steer you away from playing a stereotype. It also helps those of us who are not Tom Cruise to find joy in our work when we get a job that is not really the one we dream about. It also brings us to the point of all art, to seek the greater and deeper truths of nature and humanity. This kind of work is a beautiful process of digging deeply into the human condition to discover the contradictions, struggles and flaws in all of us. The audience lives vicariously through the characters they watch. They see reflections in their own lives and the lives of those around them in those figures on the stage and screen. Try playing the role of the Soldier in Sarah Kane's "Blasted" *without* doing this kind of work. All you will end up with is an unwatchable monster. But that monster is trapped in a world he cannot escape. And that unwatchable monster commits suicide in front of us all.

Often the depth of the character is most evident when they are silent. When they speak they are usually trying to promote a persona of themselves in order to convince the other character to give them their Objective, except in moments of great emotional conflict. Their private, silent moments of disharmony usually reveal their deepest truths. It is here that gesture in the theatre becomes highly important. On the screen it is in the eyes and through the actor's ability to triangulate the character's deeper motives. Poor actors who cannot do this will resort to one of two things. They will rattle the lines off very quickly, even cutting over the other person so that there are as few moments of listening for their character as possible. This is the "acting is doing" motif gone horribly wrong. My character must constantly be speaking or filling any voids with some kind of action or they will cease to be relevant! Not so. The other thing the poor actor does is think about the wrong thing, or worse think about nothing, in those moments of quiet and listening. On screen it is as obvious as the sky is blue. Someone once said to me of Keanu Reeves, "I like his films. But sometimes there just seems to be nothing going on in there!" Yup. That's what happens when you haven't specifically solved the deep motivating factors for your character, when you don't know what you want the audience to see, when you don't know what to have going on internally in order for it to be evident, and when you don't know how to triangulate it if you have found it. It ends up looking like a pregnant pause in the editing instead of a moment that reveals something about your character's inner life. You will notice in soap opera that these moments of revelation rarely happen during the scenes. No time is allowed for them. Then, at the end of the scene the shot will linger on an actor who is then meant to somehow portray some inner meaning after the other character has gone. (Little secret, I make sure I bring those moments of revelation into the scenes themselves. Trouble is then that the editor more often than not chops them out, not recognizing their importance.) Sometimes an actor will know what she wants the audience to see, not fully own it and demonstrate is as a generalized emotional state in that moment of quiet. That comes across as false also. The camera is very astute. If you think it or feel it, the camera will see it. It sees right underneath your eyes. You don't have to demonstrate anything. If the director wants it revealed a little more, she will tell you so.

Now it's here, in this realm of complexity, that we find a way to separate the Alec Baldwin style of acting from the Daniel Day-Lewis style of acting. If one largely plays oneself, that undercurrent of character, that second layer of meaning, is driven by the actor himself. "Good" acting on this level is when the actor is seen to have an undercurrent of dissatisfaction or personality themselves that sits beneath the work and seems to suit it. James Dean is the original example of this. Jimmy had a very difficult childhood and upbringing that caused him, by all accounts, to carry a certain lonely dissatisfaction with him through his own life. Obviously the characters in all three of his major films, East of Eden, Rebel Without a Cause and Giant have a dissatisfaction in them that is connected to a lack of family love in the character's past and present. Jimmy's mother died when he was young. He had a poor relationship with his father and was raised by his uncle and aunt. I'm sure they did the best they could, but the yearning for mother and father does not go away. Jimmy uses this deep yearning in each of those films. It suits those films and suits those characters.

In Tom Cruise we see in his life an air of cocky confidence that is enviable if you buy it and is cringe worthy if you don't. His religious convictions through Scientology highlight these traits even more clearly. They are abundantly present in his interviews and public addresses. He carries this into his films, especially those high-flying action films like Top Gun and Mission Impossible and in other ways into films like Jerry Maguire and Rainman. Alec Baldwin has an air of a corporate leader about him and he uses it as the driving current of his acting. These are personality actors who suit certain roles that meld to some degree with their own personas. They can play them with a certain ease, because the driving character traits are already there. They've carved out a lucrative career by creating a niche for themselves.

However, we know other actors less well because they do not play up to the Hollywood star system quite so much and so they invent the undercurrent or drive of their character as an artistic choice that is probably nothing to do with their own personality. Note the work of Philip Seymour Hoffman. Perhaps some of it is relatable. Perhaps certain elements of their own past or personality can be brought to bear, but it doesn't matter if these things are not present in their own psyche because they have the artistic powers to create whatever landscape of personality and the levels of it that they want through their own creative processes and technique. And they can do it convincingly.

As such you might notice that Daniel Day-Lewis and Phillip Seymour-Hoffman engage in less interviews and repartee with the public. We see them rarely unless they are promoting a film. They value their privacy and seem to shun the idea of being a product. We cannot equate their performances to their own personalities because we don't know them all that well. When we do rarely see them in interviews it is clear that they seem to be nothing like the characters they play, where as you could imagine Tom blasting his way out of the talk show studio with a grenade. They create their characters from the ground up and in all of the layers of complexity. Their craft is more like a trade in which they can adapt their materials and skills to create characters that do not exist. Essentially they build new things that haven't been seen before. They do not assume that half of the character already exists in the self. They look for the entire character by artistic and imaginative means.

Again, neither way of working is right or wrong. However you can see when something seems to be going wrong. Again, not wishing to be overly critical of anyone, Orlando Bloom brings Orlando Bloom to all the characters he plays. However for me personally, that is not enough. He is pretty and it's from there that his "good screen looks" are meant to carry him all the way through the performance of a lead role. Even his name suggests the personality he portrays. Orlando, the great romantic lead in As You Like It... blooming like a flower. However, on screen it often comes across as vacuous when Orlando relies on it. In life, Daniel Day-Lewis and Philip Seymour Hoffman could never compete in the prettiness stakes with Orlando Bloom. They are attractive in their own personal ways in life, but they bring something to the screen that Orlando either cannot, or chooses not to bring, and that's the multi-layered complexity of the characters they play. They have the technique to create those layers and are not satisfied to simply bring themselves and their own dissatisfactions, histories and personalities to the work. I don't know for sure of course, but listening to Daniel Day-Lewis in his interview with Parkinson he says that he finds his middle-class Englishness rather uninteresting. As such he looks for characters that are extremely different to him, exotic in some way and as such inspiring and interesting. That to me seems to suggest that Daniel does not *want* to get up there and play himself. His job is to create the full and layered life of a new human being, the character. These actors are still considered attractive, but for different reasons. They are attractive because of their fearlessness and their artistic abilities.

I hear so many actors complain that they can't get work because they are not pretty enough. What they are really saying is, "it would be so much easier if I was pretty because I could just play myself and people would be happy to watch me and I would get work". Well, you are what you are. You can't change that and all the plastic surgery and boob-jobs in the world are not going to solve it for you. You will end up looking plastic and your chest will look like it's had a boob job done to it, but there's a million pretty people out there looking for those roles. There are only a handful of people in the world who can do what Daniel and Philip do, and they can only do those things because they have committed themselves to becoming masters of the art of acting.

That said let's not forget that most action films and romantic comedies don't require that level of artistry in the acting. Looking pretty and saying the lines believably is for the most part all that is required and probably all that is expected of you. If you do this deeper work while working on a soap opera you might find yourself getting odd looks from other people working on it. If that's the kind of work you want sure, make sure you look your best, get some basic screen training so nothing sounds contrived and away you go. No? No, of course not. Those roles have been sewn up by pretty actors who have been "discovered". Why can't you get discovered? Maybe your uncle isn't a Hollywood star. Maybe you weren't sitting in the same bar as someone at the right time. Maybe agents won't take you on so that you can get the chance to prove yourself? Maybe you didn't have sex with the right person. Or maybe you did and then they sniffed what you were up to and decided not to help you out after all. Humiliating isn't it? What school do you go to, to find out how to do all that? I don't know. I'm sure they're out there, but I don't know and for the purpose of writing this book at least, I don't care. Everything I've just written is the epitome of what Stanislavski railed against in those opening pages of An Actor Prepares; people serving themselves for self-gain in a world of grotesque ego. It's not new. It's been going on for centuries. Fat businessmen sleazed backstage and had sex with the actresses who were told they had to because those businessmen would then be funding the next season for the theatre. Actors and actresses seduced lonely millionaires for their dosh and left them high and dry. It's a sick world out there people, and despite all of Stanislavski's attempts to change it over a hundred years ago, the theatre and now film still draws parasites who suck the life out of their environment before moving on to their next victim.

Now that's the bitter and twisted way to think about the business out there. Many actors will launch into a tirade like that and you can trust me that their bitterness is evident in their work and in their personalities. However, no matter how angry and frustrated we might get, the truth is actually a little different. Having trained actors for twenty years now, I have discovered something interesting about the agents, casting agents and directors working in the business. They actually *do* want to discover new talent. Casting is an art in itself and to cast a TV show, movie or play badly could be the difference between success and failure. So yes, they do rely on actors who have already proven themselves. They are, hopefully, safe bets, but to find the new sensation that will propel the ratings through the roof is always in the mind of the casting agent or director. I find that some casting agents and casting directors come along to see the various plays and showcases that my students and I open up to the public. I have a personal and friendly relationship with them. They are good, decent people and as far as I know they do not think about casting you contingent on how you performed in the sack. There are generally two reasons why actors end up crying foul about the industry and not being able to get work in it. Number one, they have not trained and they are not good enough. I often think of it as akin to professional soccer. Every kid out there wants to be Wayne Rooney and earn thousands a week running around a football pitch. But Wayne Rooney is naturally talented and intricately skilled. He trains *every day*. As a kid he devoted every spare second to kicking a ball. Have you done this as an actor? There are thousands, indeed millions of want-to-be stars all over the world. Are you better than them? Can you hold your own with the best actors in the world?

The second reason is that casting people do not know who you are. How can you get cast in something if they don't know who you are? You need to contact them. Send in your biog and photo and follow it up with a call. In this day and age they will want to see you act, so you need a showreel or to get yourself on stage and invite them to come. Now if you want to put yourself on stage in something, and if you want to put a showreel together, point two adds up to point one. You had better be bloody excellent. There is an ocean of showreels out there. Yours needs to grab the attention of the agent or director or whoever *immediately*. It needs to be enthralling and stunning and it needs to bring all your skills to the fore. Does it draw the viewer in? Does it show that you can bring the viewer into the inner, loneliness of the lead character? Is it filled with the essence of the character, rolling on a river of sensations? Or is it an actor trying to make it sound natural when you're not really sure of the words? Is it an actor taking a generalized, labeled emotion like anger or sadness and trying to show that they can "do anger" or cry convincingly? Ninety-nine percent of the actors out there can do that. Is it an actor scared of the camera, trying to ignore it rather than communicate with it?

If they don't get back to you or they don't come to see you, there are two reasons for that too. They are not interested in you, meaning they don't think you're good enough. Or they're just too damned busy, which is usually the case. If they don't think you're good enough, try again. If they're too damn busy, be understanding and patient and they will appreciate that. If you are trying to get an agent, there might be one more reason. They might have twenty girls on their books already who are your age and your height and your weight, and sure your showreel is ok, but its not better than those other girls and there's no point taking you on because they won't be able to get you work anyway.

It's just business. Many times my actors have been seen in a production or a showcase and been picked up by a TV show or an agent or a director from another theatre. Admittedly it's not as often as I, or they would like, but industry professionals do make the effort. They're not out to get you.

The point of that great big rant is that your ability to create characters and reveal multiple levels of meaning in complex acting is going to make casting people sit up and listen. That's what they're looking for, especially if they're casting a new TV drama, major film or a play written by a good writer. Good writing *needs* good actors. Poor acting will kill good writing. Good actors can make poor writing work, but it doesn't work the other way. In our acting, on the level we will now hopefully stay on, acting requires an approach, a system, a technique, whatever word you want to use to describe what it is you do from the moment the script arrives in your hand to the moment you step out on stage or in front of the camera. We know that we can rely on certain basic tools handed down from Stanislavski, Meisner, Adler, Chekhov and others. You will find which of those tools works the best for you. We know that from there we go into a world of exploration of the character that requires more than those basic tools that were designed for the purpose of simplification. We can no longer rely on the Objective because, as obvious and effective as it is, two problems arise. The first is that the way I might pursue an Objective may not be the same as the way the character in the play pursues the Objective. As such the actor cries, "I wouldn't do that! I don't understand this behavior! Therefore I can't play this part". Perhaps you can solve this by taking the Given Circumstances into account in more detail. Sure, that might work. You can go about developing the character and trying to think and feel yourself into someone else's way of looking at the world and try it again that way. That might work too, however it does require a lot of concentration and a huge imaginative leap from one place to another. Problem is, you don't know exactly where that other place is. You're not sure where you are going to land, so you are trying desperately to "stay in character" and at the same time trying to chart the trajectory of where you're taking the character. It's one of the great paradoxes of acting and indeed all the arts, trying to stay immersed and at the same time keeping an eye on the technical development of the work. You can either close your eyes, put the brush to the canvas and trust your instincts, or you open them and rely on the technical accuracy of your training. There is a way of doing both that brings in a third eye that watches over the work, not unlike Chekhov's "higher ego" concept. Again, this might work, but again might not.

Another option is to stick to Stanislavski's logic about the way in which he looked at the functioning world around him in order to reproduce a functioning real world on the stage. Here's the second problem with the singular Objective. If you think about it, in life we rarely want one thing only. In The Art of Acting I wrote about Multiple Objectives at length, but I will just reiterate here for those who have not read it. If you stop to think about what's going on inside of you right now, you have a few different desires going on. One is that you want to read this book, but you may also have something else you should be doing and so a certain, small percentage of your brain knows you should be doing your accounts or something. Perhaps you are getting bored with this book and are wanting, to some degree, to put it down and give up on it, but the greater part of your brain is encouraging you to keep at it in the hope it might enlighten something for you. Perhaps you are a little hungry. You want food, but you want to finish this page first. Perhaps you want to keep reading, know you should be doing your accounts and god damn it now you're hungry too. In life we are often being pulled in two or more directions at the same time. If your character is in any way well written, he or she will be too. Look at Nina in that last scene of the Seagull. Look at Hamlet in… well just about every scene! Great writers play with this stuff all the time. Lesser writers don't and you end up with a fairly flat character. As I said earlier, you can still discover depth in anything. The smallest clue can open up a cave of discovery. Great writers however fill their work with these levels of paradox, contradiction and struggle in their characters because it is deeply human to be in a state of contradiction. When a great actor who knows how to plumb the depths of these layers of contradiction meets a piece of great writing, great things happen. Thing is, you have to know how to find that landscape, and once you've found it, know what to do with it. This is the whole point of this thing we call "advanced training" as opposed to "foundation training" or no training at all where one relies purely on instinct, which when sharp works brilliantly, and when blunt causes frustration.

Have you ever gone to see an amateur production of something like Death of a Salesman? In Ireland amateur theatre is often excellent. It's convincing and enthralling. That said, no matter how convincing and enthralling it may seem to be, no matter how emotionally genuine, there's often something missing and we as audience members know something wasn't right but can't really put our finger on what that something was. Biff and Happy and their sad dad seemed to be missing something.

Perhaps that "something" is this extraordinary layering of meaning that is written in by the playwright, with the hope that a fine actor will find it. Stanislavski wrote and talked a great deal about the "inner life" of the character. Again, as with much of Stanislavski's work this term has been misconstrued. Many Stanislavski teachers will tell you that the inner life is the character's emotions. Not so. The inner life of a character is the constant churning, turning turmoil of conflicted desires and energies that are going on in all of us. Secondly to that, the inner life is seen on the surface of the character only in their private moments, or moments of total emotional abandon, which as we know from life, are extremely rare. In the normal process of trying to solve his core problem in the play, the character usually keeps that true turmoil within them hidden.

Now here's the interesting paradox that is peculiar only to the arts of theatre and film. That deep human turmoil is there and the act of hiding it from the other character actually allows it to be seen by the audience. There is nothing more bizarre if you think about it. One character is hiding some deep guilt from the other character, yet we the audience know something is wrong with them even if we the audience don't yet know why the character is feeling guilty. Some amateur actors, and of course unschooled professionals, see that the character has done something to be ashamed of so they demonstrate that shame to the audience and all the while the audience is meant to accept that the other character isn't noticing it. The confident, trained actor will demonstrate nothing, but develop that specific inner turmoil and place it in his or her own gut somewhere. This actor will trust that he or she need not do anything more than let it be there while that conversation takes place with the other character. This actor can be in character, smile through a discussion about the weather or whatever the text is and at the same time have that turmoil churning away within, confident that audience can sense it, but the other character believably cannot. A fantastic modern example of course is Bryan Cranston's Walter White in Breaking Bad.

This, of course, is the way we behave in life all the time. We do not spill our deepest problems out to everybody, in fact usually to nobody. We keep these things hidden under a polite façade that gets us through our day. Nobody notices what's really going on underneath. However on the screen or on the stage, the audience is actually looking for it. They become your mother who knows well that something is up with you when you come to visit, even if you're chatting away about the weather and baking cakes. They might not know academically the structure and machinery of drama, but ever since they were kids they have been watching movies, TV shows and plays in which the lead character at least will have to deal with some inner struggle as well as a more obvious outer problem. In a kid's cartoon some character will have to save the world (outer problem) and have to struggle with their deep inner fear of failure, for example (inner problem). The audience knows it and so they expect it. Therefore while this hypothetical character chats away to another character, the audience are actually looking, albeit subconsciously, for the inner conflict and turmoil.

And here's the interesting thing that makes this work so important. That inner landscape actually *is* more than half the character. The outer façade is most of the other half, and the way in which the character hides the inner self is the rest.

1. Inner (hidden) landscape
2. Outer (apparent) landscape
3. The individual way the character balances 1. and 2.

This is the personality of we humans in life, and the character on the stage. Without discovering this, you won't know where you're trying to land. So let's dig into this now in some depth.

The Possible Someone

THE INNER LANDSCAPE

As I've said, within us all is a very specific inner life that makes me me and makes you you. Stop and have a listen to it sometime. You have doubts, fears, inhibitions, all bouncing against certain assurances and confidences. They are the results of your circumstances, memory, experiences and your physical reality.

Stanislavski asked his actors to invent entire histories for their characters that were not necessarily prescribed by the author in order to bring a very intricate inner landscape onto the stage with them. He asked this of the leads and also of the most minor of characters. A whole lot of hard work for no result I hear you say? That's arguable, but it was certainly an interesting experiment. The fact that the character got lost in the supermarket when he was five years old and couldn't find his mommy may not be relevant when playing Rosencrantz. You've invented it. It has nothing to do with Rosencrantz. However, when you read that play something about Rosencrantz's words and behavior led you to a thought; an idea that this behavior is not just superfluous and haphazard on the part of Shakespeare. It's grounded, rooted in a personality that has been developed for a long time. So when the Queen takes his hand and asks him earnestly to find out what's wrong with her son, something twigs in him. He does not suddenly remember running around a supermarket, roaring in tears being pursued by strangers who are only trying to help but that he thinks are monsters trying to abduct him, but that mother looking for her lost son makes a friend become a spy. It makes sense. It is more than duty to a Queen. It is duty to a mother. The moment is enhanced. The surface of a spy kissing the ass of the

Queen in order to get into her favors goes away and something new, interesting and deep replaces the cliché.

Hence the inner landscape affects the outer landscape. Beautiful moments of true theatre reveal themselves in the outer behavior because the inner is full and creatively built. To put it bluntly, we are looking at *real* people instead of "characters" who don't really exist and seem to have just arrived out of the sky half there and half still in the sky; half the actor and half Rosencrantz; half developed, quickly developed, born of cliché.

Yes, these are choices that will dictate the behavior of the character on the stage or screen. There will be communication with a director on these choices and the actor must be prepared to face a director who just wants the first clichéd option. In a way that's okay too. You have to work, so work. Hopefully, sooner than later, your choices will be respected and considered. Once they are and interesting moments begin to get kept by smarter directors and editors, ears will prick up and you will be called upon to work by more people who want that level of artistic thought and creativity.

The inner landscape of a character is not a purely psychological exercise. Our bodies are what was given to us when we entered the world and also a result of our growing, our environment, and of thoughts and feelings. Yes, the way you thought and felt as you grew is manifest right now in your body and the way you hold it and use it in your day-to-day life. Your "tempo rhythm" as Stanislavski calls it, your posture, your gestures, the amount of eye contact you maintain in conversations, the entire package that is you physically is a result of a long prelude of development. What is that package for your character? Irrelevant I hear again? Sure. If you like. Just be you and say the lines so they can be heard. There is no character. It has no personality or inner existence other than your own.

Or does it?

How many performances of a great play have you seen in which the actor has used the text as a vehicle for his own ego? I've seen literally hundreds of them. And maybe it's just me but when I see Hamlet or Glengarry Glenross or View from the Bridge and have to watch an actor skate over opportunities that are there for all to see, it begins to grate on the bones. Tell your own story somewhere else. I've come to see Hamlet, Roma, Eddie.

The Inner landscape is also filled with many wonderful bits of information that again might directly affect the outer behavior. Appetites about sex, booze, food, moral tendencies towards adultery, manipulation, blackmail, may again fuel a moment of excellence that would otherwise have gone by the by. Look hard at the text of the great writers, take their clues and have your own fun. You may or may not use your fun choices, but you are getting to know the "possible someone" that is the character in an intimate and enjoyable way. Who knows where it will lead?

Perhaps there is no character. So make one. Have fun making this "possible someone".

To put it in somewhat childish terms, The Inner Landscape is the *kind* of person your character is on the inside. Everything from their past, their political views, their attitudes and opinions and their doubts about all those things are housed here. Get to know it!

The Possible Someone

OUTER LANDSCAPE

So if the inner landscape of the character is this struggle within between various conflicting forces, the outer landscape is the struggle externally to achieve the Objective or solve the Core Problem, or both. It's what the audience literally sees, not so much what they sense and perceive.

Let's take Eddie in A View from the Bridge as an example. Here is a man who walks into his house after having grassed on his niece's boyfriend partly at least because he has feelings for his niece that are confusing to him. He's filled with internal struggle with himself and his actions and declares in an argument with his wife that he wants his respect. The inner landscape obviously is going to dictate how he behaves in his outer actions. He knows well that he really doesn't deserve that respect, and like all people who want respect when they know they have not earned it, loses his cool and demands it and eventually ends up in tears. The big dog becomes beaten by the inescapable truth of his circumstances. No matter how hard he pretends to have done right, no matter how much of a front of manliness he tries to maintain, no matter how much he tries to justify himself and his actions, his inner, human self knows what he has done. Again, the actor can know these things and pretend. However the deep pain that Eddie is going through is incredibly complex.

When we experience these kinds of struggles in life it is our human facility, working through a complex matrix of thoughts and feelings that determines certain behaviors. We have a front or façade that we show to the world. So does Eddie. What exactly is going on underneath it? And how long does the front remain solid in the face of the truth that is bubbling beneath? It is achievable to pretend it all, of course. However it is only when the actor lends himself, that is the actor's own human facility, to that intense matrix of confused feelings, that surprising behavior is revealed. Behavior that was previously not considered appropriate or possible now becomes an epiphany to the director, the actors and even the playwright. Artistic possibilities are born and on the camera they are captured whilst on the stage they are developed and harvested from performance to performance. In rehearsals we can sit around a table all day discussing these dynamics, trying to logically put them in place and shed some light on them, however it is better to just do it. Let the actor understand the text, get up on the floor and behave according to the impulses that are born from his understanding. Discover these things not as intellectuals trying to solve an equation, but as actors and artists allowing the work to some extent to create itself as we go. Forget about blocking. More than likely it will solve itself if the actor also has a basic knowledge of stagecraft or preferably an understanding of the easy power of triangulation.

It is true that the Objective is all-important. We can never lose sight of it, no matter how intricate our inner landscape becomes. The Objective stops the possibility of self-indulgence. This is not my time to be an actor. This is Eddie's time to be revealed.

Again we come across this question of the character. If I am doing all this stuff, am I me filtering Eddie's circumstances and problems through me? Or am I Eddie? And when, if ever, do I *become* Eddie and stop being me?

The answer to that is up for debate. First of all, if I am owning and processing Eddie's issues using my own faculties as a human and as an artist, one might argue that the moment I feel a feeling that is not my own but based on Eddie's stuff, and allow my behavior to be dictated by that, I am no longer me. These are not my problems. I am not bringing my problems into the play. I am setting my own stuff aside to allow Eddie's stuff in. Once it is in, I am not checking my behavior and pre-empting my reactions based on what I think I *might* do, or even based on what I think Eddie *should* do. I am in another place altogether. It is not some kind of strange, magical place, it is a logical place based on the work we have just discussed. Logical it is. Artistic it is too. Why? Because like high art in any other medium, there is a place in which I do not have to worry about my technique, check my work while acting, question my worthiness or worry about the audience or the critics. I just stay in that intricate world of inner and outer conflicts and cut the cord and behave. I let action be free, based on the work I've done. I let moments that may seem wrong or inappropriate have their moment. In fact, I'm not letting anything happen. Those things are happening without me. All I have to do is be there.

Once physical characterization has been worked into the process, costumes, accents, weight, gait, whatever is relevant to Eddie, and that work is married with the rest of the work, audiences suspend their disbelief and allow themselves to "believe" that they are watching Eddie, not some actor pretending to be Eddie. They become absorbed in his story. They root for him, or against him. They play the game of make-believe with us. Like children listening to Jack and the Beanstalk being read to them, they know that Daddy is reading words from a book. They know there is no such thing as Giants, or even Jack for that matter and nor is there any such thing as Eddie. They are not stupid and we are not pretending they are. But they go with us. They follow the story. They know, albeit subconsciously that we are talking about poverty and bravery and desire and vulnerability and various other thematic ideas. And when the story is over, it lives in their minds as they lie in their beds and drift off to sleep, reliving it, retelling it to themselves, wondering. Eddie may not exist any more than Jack or his beanstalk, but Eddie means something very human and they follow his experience of struggle and learning. Therefore our job is to find him, as if he does exist, because an idea of Eddie is a phantom that has only academic meaning. A physically, vocally, psychologically unique Eddie in front of unique human beings in an audience is a human exchange that means a great deal. We call it theatre.

You see, in a story or a book, the reader or listener envisages the characters. On the stage we have the luxury of actually building them and putting them in front of the audience. *This* is your Eddie for tonight's production. It may not be the same as the last Eddie you saw when you saw this play fifteen years ago. This is tonight's Eddie. We have found this Eddie carefully and joyously. We hope it gives you joy too.

When Eddie seems to be existing without the actor manipulating him for his own egotistical ends, we in the audience follow Eddie. We listen to his story and get involved in the communion of theatre. We haven't been fooled or manipulated. We have chosen, confident in the skills before us, to allow ourselves to be told a story.

As such, I would propose that this is the character and this is the time that the character is truly fully formed and self-aware. It is the moment when the work is complete in all its facets and the actor is allowing all that work to function freely, allowing the character to move and behave according to itself. The hand of the painter is moving freely allowing the picture to be revealed, not judging it, not checking it. We see the outer behavior and we sense all the wonderful confusion and complexity that is being hidden and slowly revealed from within.

PSYCHOLOGICAL, PHYSICAL AND EMOTIONAL "ONENESS"

Previously I have used the words psychological, emotional and physical to describe the complete work of acting and characterization. As you can see from the last few pages, these terms are not good enough anymore. Perhaps they are all we have, but they do not encompass what we mean when we act and they can be so easily misunderstood that they can easily lead an actor into an abyss of mistakes. "Damn, this isn't working! The emotions aren't there! I know. I'll get really angry!" But of course you're not getting "really angry". You are clutching at a generalized emotion to try to fool the audience that you are in the right place. If you yell and shout and cry loud enough for long enough they will applaud your energy and maybe even call it good acting. You hope. "I am thinking about that speech coming up in Act II. Damn I am not in the right psychological place. What will I do? Try to "think" like the character." Ain't going to work either. "I don't know what to do with my hands. I haven't done my physical homework. I'll shove them in my pockets". Awful trap after awful trap.

The idea that we are somehow divided as humans between our psychological, emotional and physical selves is archaic. In acting and indeed in any art it is poisonous. You cannot solve these things for the character one at a time in some kind of systematic way. You can try, and I'm not debasing approaches based on this thinking, but try to tell me when one stops and another starts? You can't. Emotions are based on endorphins and chemicals and reactions to the outer world that are physical. Psychologically we attempt to lasso them and control them in some way and when that doesn't work we get tired physically and entirely different emotions are going on before we even stop to realize it. Human beings are a mess. What we are looking to discover in our character is the wonderful mess that is them. What mess am I playing today? What confusion and discontent and contradiction am I going to let house itself in me when "action" is called? How can I judge and preempt the behavior that will result from being immersed in that wonderful mess? I can't. I have to let the mess rule the work. Scary thought isn't it?

What a glorious mess is Eddie, Hamlet, Ophelia, Nina and Constantine, Trigorin and Arkadina, Uncle Vanya, Ivanov and Sasha, Astrov and Sonya, Daniel Plainview, Truman Capote, Blanch, Marlene and Joyce and all the rest! How do we begin to penetrate that mess?

Firstly, we must understand that we are all a mess too. Then we as actors must put our own mess aside and let another mess in. That's the discipline. In our structured world of routine, taxes and breakfasts at seven am and the nine-to-five corporate world that most people live in or are controlled by in one way or another, the actor must be able to glorify the mess of the character within the structure of their circumstances. The actor must *live* the mess of someone else, the character, and then go back to their own. For artists who may not have structures, who are ruled by impulses and dreams, we find the subject of our art and that *becomes* the structure. The actor then becomes deeply in tune with the human mess before him. He enters into the mess of another in an all absorbing and full way. That's the never-ending work of the actor as an artist.

For many actors, life *without* a subject to work on is often very difficult and sometimes quite unbearable.

Once a great teacher of mine listened to me whine about the nature of things for some time. My discontent about this and that theatre and this and that casting agent, lack of money, lack of recognition; this rant went on for some time. I bored the poor man to tears. Eventually he said, "Are you an artist?" "Of course," I replied. "Then start to behave like one." And he walked away. Once that thought went in I realized that all my whining and all the things I'd been whining about were distractions from the one thing that I knew to be true, that I was an artist and had an awful lot of artistic things to do. I hadn't asked for it. It was just the fact of things.

Things are a mess. People are a mess. Characters are a wonderful mess too. So lets find our way to them, to the third place, to acting with abandon. Let's find our way to art. The world in which we are trying to practice that art is a mess and as much as we can work towards fixing it, let's forget about it for now and concentrate on achieving artistically and evolving.

So no matter how we divide and subdivide our work, let's remember that we are looking for the "oneness" of the character. If we feel the need to talk about the character's "emotional life", "psychological life" and "physical life, that's all well and good as long as we keep our eye on the prize which is the mess, the oneness and the true, congealed essence of the character.

The Possible Someone

EMOTION

There's a TV show here in Ireland called "The Voice of Ireland". My kids love to watch it. Singers come in and audition for a panel of judges who then build their own team of singers and become their "mentors" (although they have no experience of teaching singers). They then compete and get knocked out by the audience vote until one singer is left standing. This singer is that year's "voice of Ireland". It's a pretty vacuous idea, but makes for some interesting entertainment. One of the judges is one of the Corr sisters from the band The Corrs. I don't like their music much myself, but that's just a personal response. This judge pretty much always charts her decisions on whether or not "the emotion" was there in a particular performance. "There was no emotion", she cries. "I'm not feeling the emotion". And conversely, "there was emotion! I really felt it."

What the hell does that mean? A song, like a play or a poem or any other piece of written literature is a narrative, and usually quite a simple one. Boy meets girl, boy loses girl and so on. The tune itself lends certain emotional weight to the thing. Minor chords usually give darker, more brooding atmospheres, while major chords are a bit more happy clappy and give us a lift. So what is the singer's job? To sing clearly and hit the tune accurately. Can the singer add emotion? Yes, by "sounding emotional" when singing it. Should the singer get emotional or fake that emotion? If you actually get emotional, it is very difficult to continue singing. Try singing when you are crying. It's almost impossible. Crying causes your tear ducts to swell, a lump to develop in your throat, your nose to run and your breathing to become irregular.

Much the same can be said of acting, except that in acting you can continue to act whilst crying because the time you need to take a breath, to wipe the tears or snot away will often actually lend a certain reality to the moment of high emotion. It's not singing, it's behavior, and those gestures and necessities of trying to deal with tears are believable. We've all been there and so the audience recognizes the struggle of crying. Can you sort it out and shake it off before the next scene when the character is no longer upset? Now that's the question.

So Ms Corr is looking for something. What is that? Does she want the singer to be emotional? Does she want the singer to fake it and *sound* emotional? Or does she not really care about either of those things as long as she, the audience member, feels emotional? It's a very odd note to give a singer unless you actually explain what you mean by it. Ironically I just watched an episode last night in which a singer who was not accepted last year came back and performed again to try to get in. She didn't get in. The panel were gobsmacked that she had come back and pretty much done the same thing again without taking on their notes about "emotion" given to her the year before. Of course she did the same thing again and of course she had no "emotion" because she had no idea what these people were talking about.

So why am I going on about that? Because such is the confusion surrounding emotion in actor training. Again, much of this comes from the incredibly hostile reaction to Strasberg's work and the concept of Emotion Memory. More often than not these hostile reactions come from a complete misunderstanding of what Method is, but let's not get into that again. Let's get into emotion in light of these inner and outer landscapes because you can solve a lot of your emotional landscape by solving those first. Remember now that we are talking about actual emotion, not sensations.

Let's assume then that characters in general are going about trying to achieve something, either an Objective or the solving of a core problem. At what point then does the character get emotional? Have a look in the script. It's usually prescribed reasonably clearly by the writer. It will be once, maybe twice for the protagonist and antagonist and probably not at all for the smaller roles. So Hamlet loses the plot at Ophelia's grave, his uncle begs for the mercy of heaven for is rank offence of killing the king, his mother cannot look his son in the eye when she is forced to compare her previous husband with the one she has replaced him with and it is arguable that Ophelia might become emotional when lamenting her father's death as she passes flowers to the others. But even that one is arguable, because you have to remember that at this point she might be insane. It all depends on how you want to play it. So in a very long play with many, many characters, there is really very few moments of total emotional abandon. You could take any of them in another direction if you wanted to.

Think of the story of Christ. When does Jesus get emotional? Only twice in his entire life. Once when he trashes the temple market because of the blasphemous way it is being used by the Romans and money exchangers, and when he cries out on the cross, "My God, my God, why have you forsaken me!" in a moment of utter loss and injustice. The rest of his life is the pursuit of an enormous and very complex Objective, to change the thinking of human kind. He can't do that by being hopelessly emotional all day.

Okay. So we can get some idea from the text, but nothing is nailed down (pardon the pun). If nothing is nailed down, how can we make any decision? Let's ask a simple question based on that last example of the story of Jesus. When do we get emotional in life? More specifically, when do we let the emotions that we usually keep contained out and into the public arena? Very rarely. All right. But when?

We become sad and cry or become extremely angry and perhaps shout usually only on three occasions in our lives. Number one: Loss or the threat of loss. Number two: Injustice or the threat of injustice. Number three: A combination of one and two.

Go to the play then and ask yourself where the character experiences one of these three moments. Those are the ones that *might* require an emotional outpouring. The rest of the time the character may be feeling a mass of confused emotions, but in order to try to achieve the Objective or solve the core problem, the character will contain them or deal with them in other ways. Your character could not possibly achieve anything if he or she is pouring emotional borsch out into the world from moment to moment. You couldn't achieve anything in your life if you behaved like that either. No one would want to deal with you. You would probably be clapped in a loony bin.

As such, the confusion surrounding Emotion Memory, Method and all the arguments about emotion in acting are predicated on a misconception that the actor is meant to "show the character's emotion" from moment to moment in the play. As such you might be unfortunate enough see a production of Hamlet in which the actor pours grief and angst all over the stage for three hours. Have you ever heard a director say to an actor, "It's all on one level"? That's usually what's going on. The actor is playing what he thinks is the right emotion all day long. It's tiring to do, tiring to watch and uninteresting and unconvincing.

The character is and must always be active, and I don't mean by running around all over the place; active by going for an Objective; active by trying to solve a problem. Therefore, when the character does become emotional it is because something has happened that he or she no longer has control over. That is, he or she sees that the Objective is no longer achievable or that the Core Problem is unsolvable.

Let's look at a few famous examples. The character of Hitler in "Downfall" loses his rag only when the Objective of winning the war has been clearly taken from his control. Nick Nolte's wonderful moment on the stairs in "Lorenzo's Oil" when he knows that his child is terminally ill and there is nothing in his power that he can do to help him. Sean Penn in "Mystic River" when he knows his daughter's body is in the pit and despite all of his gangland connections and tough-guy power can do nothing to wind back the clock. Great injustice, terrible loss, or a combination of both. Everything else is the character actively trying to deal with the loss or correct the injustice. Notice the way Sean reins in that seething emotion in other parts of the movie; when being questioned by the cops, when talking on the porch to his old friend. The emotion is there, bubbling and ready to overflow, but it is contained almost completely. That "everything else" may have huge emotional life driving it, but without a control on it, nothing will get done and there will be no chance of any Objective being pursued or achieved. The audience will notice that and give up on the whole game.

There is one other moment both in life and in drama where tears come to us and that is a moment of great achievement or change. When David Helfgot finally plays Rachmaninov publically for the first time in decades and receives a standing ovation in the film "Shine", Geoffrey Rush allows the tears to flow. It is a moment of immense, life affirming metamorphosis, and to my memory, I don't think he cries at any other time in the film. These are moments when the impossible Objective has been achieved and the impossible problem has been solved. Essentially, it's the "happy ending".

A great example is "Lincoln". Here I am only judging this from my own experience, but tears came to my eyes when the thirteenth amendment abolishing slavery was passed. Huge moment of metamorphosis, impossible Objective achieved, insurmountable problem solved. Then when Lincoln is shot, one would think that would be the moment for tears and there was none. Great loss and injustice, but the moment of triumph trumped it. If those two moments had been combined… that is, Lincoln is killed before the bill is passed, or just moments before so that he never gets to see the fruits of his labors, now that would have been something. But that's a stretch too far because it's not history.

I once played a small role in a film in which the lead was a female character who had been raped at a cocaine-fueled high-society party. She cried from beginning to end in that movie and, for me anyway, it was practically unwatchable and unbelievable. What led the actress to think that was the right choice to make?

In "The Art of Acting" I introduced the triad notion of "Sympathy, Empathy and Third Place". If my character has been raped, sure I might feel sympathy for her terrible experience and cry *for her*. If I empathize, I put myself in her shoes and wonder how I might feel. And yes, I cry, perhaps out of the fear of having to go through that ordeal. Perhaps I too have been raped in the past. I know how she feels and so the memory of my own experience causes me to cry. However, the actor cannot operate from either of those starting points. They might be helpful in coming to an understanding of the Given Circumstances, but after that there is an entire script there with an imperative Objective and a massive Core Problem that the character needs to try to achieve and solve. What that actress did was "correctly" find the emotion of distress that might be experienced during the rape or even in the shower afterwards, but then ignored the Objective and the Core Problem and demonstrated that emotion all the way through the film, in every take and every scene, in every shot and every frame, no matter what the action of that scene happened to be at the time.

The fact is we deal with shit. So does your character, no matter how difficult that shit is. We learn. So does your character. We have an internal landscape and an external one. So does your character. The notion that "good acting" is "emotional acting" doesn't hold up and never has. The actor has to play what's on the page. Yes there will be externally noticeable emotion there, but it will be at rare moments. The churning turmoil underneath the external façade (the mess), kept in check by a character determined to achieve an Objective and solve a problem is far more interesting, far more theatrical and far more dramatic.

So what do you do if like many of us, you are getting yourself small roles of messengers in films and TV series where there are no moments of high emotional abandon? Of course we all want to act well and give a good impression hoping we will impress and get more work. But there's nothing you can do. If you have a few lines and your character's Objective is to deliver a message, you can only deliver the message. Do the thing. Follow the action. That's not bad acting, that's good acting and the director will appreciate it if you create the character, put on the costume and just do it, strongly and clearly in keeping with the circumstances of that moment, preferably in one take. To spend hours wondering how you will deliver the emotion of that moment, or in some way to say the line emotionally is utterly ludicrous and will achieve you nothing. Usually if the message is of great import, as soon as it is delivered, the director will swing the camera on to the receiver of the message to get the reaction. That's where the emotion is living. So don't feel put out if the final edit doesn't focus on you. It's not about you. It's about the action and it's consequences to the main characters. It's about telling the story.

The Possible Someone

FEAR AND CONFIDENCE

So keep digging into the mess.

There are certain things that are common to all human beings and have been since we were cavemen. Let's make a list.

Sex (desire)

Addiction (Alcohol, tobacco, drugs and substance addiction)

Mental State

Physical State

Sleep

Death

Love

Hunger/Thirst

Money/Lack of Money

Ambition

Bondage/Betrayal (Injustice)

Freedom (Justice)

We all experience a grappling of some sort with one or the other of these ten things during our existence on this planet. How we manage them is the sum of us as individuals. How we manage them is almost always based on a very powerful internal struggle between two things: Fear and Confidence.

At the moment I am writing this, the nation of Ireland is weighted under the yoke of bondage and betrayal that has been brought on by corrupt financial institutions and their leaders and corrupt political parties and the leaders of those. The result has been that every citizen is laden with an enormous debt that will be passed on to their children and their children's children. Power has been wrested from the political leaders of the country and transferred to powers in European institutions in order that the enormous debt be forcibly repaid. Austerity taxes with invented names, one atop the other, pile onto the average citizen. And yet the citizen's of Ireland do nothing. They do not protest, they do not march in the streets, they do not take up arms and invade the halls of power. They roll over and take it. Why? Some have suggested that since the "Troubles" in Northern Ireland, which claimed thousands of innocent lives both north and south of the partition, an extraordinary over-reaching psychology of fear has invaded the Irish mentality. To take up arms, to walk in the streets holds deep-seated reminiscences of massacres, bludgeoning police, burned out vehicles and total fear. In other countries however, at this same moment, such as Egypt and Syria, mass revolt, civil strife and protest are not only considered acceptable, but absolutely necessary to remind those in power that the masses will not lie down and be kicked; that if the powers that be want to do something unpopular, they sure as shit better know they are going to have to answer to a lot of angry people. The culture there is born of ancient tribal struggles towards a path that most people hopefully will agree on. But of course most people don't agree on one thing and democracy, at least Western-style democracy is considered a fallacy that is hopelessly exposed to corruption, as it has been in Ireland.

Now there's a huge, political landscape upon which to consider these ideas. The point is, Ireland is *behaving* and *reacting* to austerity according to its personality and its history (theoretically). Greece and Iceland reacted in entirely different ways to the same circumstances. Their reaction to their circumstances, the way they deal with their mess defines them and tells us an awful lot about them, their history and their collective personality.

Let's look at a simple individual dynamic. A guy at a bar is attracted to a girl. He sees her talking with her friends. He wants to talk to her. It will be his fear of rejection and humiliation or his confidence that rejection and humiliation won't occur that will determine whether he goes over and talks to her. What he chooses to do of course depends on his character. He is the sum of his actions. His management of fear and confidence partly defines who he is. And just as it is with the international political example, there will be a reason behind his eventual behavior. Whether he does or doesn't go over and speak to her will be traceable back to some important event or events that happened in his past and led him to be the kind of guy he is. What "kind of guy" he is, is his "character".

Let's take a famous cinematic example. Penn, Nolte and Caviezel are playing characters caught in a famous World War II campaign in Guadalcanal in the South Pacific. They have to invade this island faced with the real probability that they will never leave it and the Imperial Japanese army will remain dug in. It would be a rare individual who would not feel the grip of fear in such a situation. Watch closely as these three astute actors cleverly pitch their performances on their character's ability to manage fear in different ways. They have, in fact, faced their fears in such a prolonged and deep way that they have worked their way out the other end of fear itself. Their behavior is now based on that process. Terrence Malick leaks lovely, subtle suggestions of their pasts to us and we get this incredibly deep sense of fully formed individuals with fully formed pasts that have brought them to this moment of intense mortality. Each of these actors has taken all those clues, despite their subtlety and added them together to create their performances.

Going back to the list, your character will more than likely be dealing with one or the other of these things in your script. What you need to work out is exactly which one it is. Once you have it, with good writing you will probably notice that more than one is at play and you will begin to create compound layering of your character. David Helfgot wants to play Rachmaninov (ambition) with a one-hundred-a-day cigarette habit (addiction) and a mental condition, and having fallen in love, and seeing the world through coke-bottle glasses (physical state). Geoffrey Rush is the artist who does the balancing, works out the measure of things and puts it all together.

Once again, with mediocre writing, you may have a little less work to do, but there will always be *some work* to do if you want to drill into the character rather than simply say the lines as yourself.

In life we suffer everything on that list at some stage or other. How we deal with them, through the lenses of fear and confidence, defines us. If you would like your character to be as complex as you or I or anyone else in the world, give them the credit of asking these questions.

Many practitioners have lampooned Stanislavski for his insistence on deep research on the part of his actors. As already discussed, at stages in his work he would have his actors write out a history of their character from birth to the present taking as much as possible from the script and logically inventing the rest. Of course all Stanislavski was trying to do was help his actors find a justification for the way their character was behaving in the script. What has made this person behave in this way? If the way you handle fear and confidence defines you to even some degree, it's probably the result of your past or your development. A knowledge of that could be enormously helpful, and could deliver a layer of characterization that will enrich your artistic creation.

COMPLEX CIRCUMSTANCES

Buddha tells us that the essential nature of the human condition is suffering, and he's probably right. Conditions aren't great, let's face it. Gravity keeps shoving us towards the ground, which is terribly tiring. Our bodies are a mass of tingling nerves that cause us to feel all sorts of unpleasant sensations like pain, hot and cold. Our bodies are soft and easily invaded by bacteria and viruses. The body ages. Eventually it will stop working altogether.

Worse again, those things which we do find pleasant like alcohol, tobacco, pot or whatever else your pleasure is, have a built in downside: addiction, hangovers, cancer, heart disease, paranoia and an overall further weakening of an already fragile organism. On top of that we have a mind that freaks out with stress and anxiety when things are going arse-ways, pumping all sorts of bizarre chemicals, hormones and endorphins around our brain and body, and a heart (for want of a better term) that feels emotions as a result of those chemicals and hormones that can be so strong that they can make us behave in ways that can even bewilder ourselves. Why did I do that? What was I thinking?

Living, when you look at what "god" or nature or whatever has given us, is virtually impossible and seems like a kind of sadistic form of torture. However there is another thing about us humans that is the savior of it all. The Buddha copped it a long time ago. We have the capacity to understand that we are suffering, that we will suffer and that there is no point in pretending that there will be a place or time where we won't suffer. Once that enlightenment takes place in the Buddhist, living becomes infinitely easier. As soon as there is any feeling of upset or pain or sickness, instead of freaking out, the Buddhist says "Of course. I have a headache because that is the nature of life. Why wouldn't I have a headache?" "Of course that person was mean to me. They are reacting to their own suffering. And I'm feeling hurt because that's life. I suffer too." Meditation helps to move the consciousness of the individual to another, deeper level in the same way that sinking deep into the water means we won't be buffeted by the big waves on the surface.

That's why it's very important for the actor to be a Buddhist. I'm joking of course. The point of all this is that the characters we play are generally not Buddhists. They are plagued with discontent and dissatisfaction, desires and needs, fragility and emotion and they react to events in very specific ways which are dependent entirely on their character and what the author has prescribed. They are on the surface of their circumstances, being buffeted by the huge waves of their highly dramatic predicament. They, like us, are trapped in a universal set of circumstances that is common to all of us. On a second level they are trapped in a specific set of circumstances that is unique to them. And thirdly they react to those circumstances in a way that is specific to them as a character. Discovering the way they react to their circumstances and deal with the big waves can help us in yet another way to individualize them.

Universal Circumstances

Personal Circumstances

Unique Response to Universal Circumstances

Unique Response to Personal Circumstances

Although I was being flippant about actors needing to be Buddhists, the actor to some extent must go on a little personal odyssey of discovery within the self and then without. And don't worry it is not dangerous and difficult as is the mistaken perception of Strasberg's work. To ask these questions of oneself is a very interesting process and makes you a better actor. How do I react to the universal circumstances of us all? How did I end up like I am? What has brought me to this moment of the present? What happened to me to make me the way I am and make me react to circumstances in certain ways? How much does fear control me? Am I heroic? Am I not? Am a little bit heroic? When I behave like an ass, do I know it and accept it or do I sense that I might have been in the wrong, ignore that sense and behave like an ass all over again? Do I enjoy seeing people succeed or hate seeing people succeed? And why? What made me like that?

The list of possible questions goes on and on and deeper and deeper like a veritable rabbit hole. It can be quite an eye opening experience. It's not quite the same as Buddhist enlightenment, but it can certainly change you. It can make you start to look at the world in another way. When someone treats you badly, for example, you don't immediately leap to an emotional response, but rather you sort of pity them and wonder what has happened to them in their past to make them behave like that.

Then something very interesting happens once your thinking has gone there. You start to think this way and ask these questions about your character. Why are they behaving this way? You start to wonder. You start to daydream about things that may have made them like that. You start to go down the rabbit hole with and for your character and then somewhere while you are falling, you move from sympathy to empathy and into the third place and you sort of join with them. You do what they do and feel what they feel and think their thoughts. It's not magic, it's acting, and the mind is perfectly capable of that imaginative leap.

Have you ever struggled to "act well"? You know something isn't right. When I see that happening on the stage or the screen it's often, I think, because the actor sees the way the character is reacting in that script and then tries to force that behavior without an understanding of where it's coming from. They are so caught up in their own problems and questions about their worth and ability, so caught up in the act of "being confused" of "struggling with the text" of "wrestling with the character" as if it's some wild horse they need to tame and sit on, that there is no way they can actually allow that character in. There's too much of the actor reacting to his own circumstances and not enough of the actor who can look at the behavior of the character in the script, ask the question of why and go down that wonderful, imaginative and creative rabbit hole. And go down it selflessly. I've said it before and I'll say it again. Acting is not about the actor. As soon as it becomes about the actor, the character will be like a bored date sitting with her head in her hand trying to stay awake while her date sits opposite her crapping on about himself with his mouth half full of steak. Essentially she's waiting for him to shut the hell up and let her in.

Many practitioners of actor training and theatre have spoken of the importance of observation of the natural world. In fact, from my laborious research I don't think I've found one that hasn't in one form or another and again they are all absolutely right. However, observing the world is one thing. Tuning into it is another. Seeing things from your own perspective and judgment is limiting. Seeing the world through subjective eyes and an open mind is something else entirely and a learning experience. To be able to accept the truth that many people don't want to accept, that we actually are animals as much as our household dog is, is a humbling and enlightening experience. "Oh animals don't have feelings. That's not emotion your dog is exhibiting. It's not capable of that. Har har har!" is ignorant. The fact is, if we look at it in any kind of logical way, animals and plants do not stress anywhere near as much as we do. They do no complicate themselves by creating currency and economic structures. They do not try to be monogamous until they go crazy with jealousy. They don't cry out and wail about death, which is the most natural thing any of us will experience in our lives. They don't rape and pillage their own environment. They just live, for the most part, in harmony with it. Who's the inferior species? We have developed complications that upset us. Therefore we are superior. I don't think so. But these complications are complicated. Therefore we are superior. Again, I don't think so, and frankly I don't think the complications are that complicated or intelligent. Rather they seem based on a system of greed and self-aggrandizement.

We need to take a good hard look at ourselves. The actor who is an artist also needs to take a good hard look at humanity. The arts are all an attempt to drill into the mystery of the human condition. If the actor is not doing something similar, then what's the actor doing? Imitating for the sake of entertainment? Showing off for the sake of self-aggrandizement? Begging for change? The actor is an artist, and a very complex one with a wonderfully complex role to play in society. Now that's a complicated task… to dig into the very fabric of why humans think they are so damn smart, amongst other things.

Your character is a human being struggling within the human circumstances imposed upon him. Dig into those universal circumstances and find out what they are *doing* to him. How is the society around him making him behave? How are his own personal circumstances and his own mess making him behave? Why is he reacting to them in the way he does?

The Possible Someone

PLACEMENT

Right. So let's get a grip on what we've discussed so far. We've worked out that Stanislavski started all of his wonderful work by looking at the natural world and asking himself how he can put something as wonderful as the actual confusing reality of being human on the stage. He broke that down into Given Circumstances and Objectives among other things before he went on to even more "other things" such as gesture and grand opera. We've looked much more deeply into that reality and broached the idea that a character is defined by its actions and behavior. To discover how to play a character we need to work out the reason behind its behavior as prescribed in the text. If we can work out what has brought the character to that point in its existence, quite simply we can work out how to *be* that person. We've looked at the actor as a human being and as an artist. We've looked at the tangible road that the actor can go down to become the character, bypassing sympathy and empathy and joining with the mess that is that character to become them in a palpable way.

The long and the short of it is, we don't actually have to act badly. We don't have to throw our hands in the air and pretend the character doesn't exist and it's all too much for our little heads to handle. We don't have to poorly demonstrate the first-choice, obvious behavior we see evident in the text, or worse, an assumption about what we thought the writer *really* meant. We can find the real human being behind that mess, behind that behavior and embody that difficult, confusing state of being so that we don't have to demonstrate anything. We are simply caught up in someone else's mess. With a little stagecraft and a little cameracraft, we can then work out how to tell that story for the audience.

The audience sees what we want them to see. If my character is lying, I can put into my own (the character's) head that I'm lying and that will leak right out into the camera or the audience without me having to demonstrate a damn thing. If my character is telling the truth, I can do the same. If I want my audience to be unsure, debating whether or not I'm lying or telling the truth during the interval, I can do that too. It's a matter of placing what I want within my head... or my heart... or my soul... or AH!!! There it is! Where does that information go? Where do I PLACE it?

It's a very difficult question to answer. It's an enigma of the imagination. Some would suggest that it is *the* question of advanced acting. What are those great actors actually doing? What's going on inside them? The answers to that vary of course. They vary from actor to actor. This is the whole crux of the Hoffman/Olivier debate. "Why don't you try acting?" But what is that? To Olivier it clearly wasn't immersing himself into the physical and psychological predicament of his character to the extent that he took that on himself. It was something else; a good guess, based on good instincts, at what the character should look and sound like and behave like, and usually it worked. Usually. In my personal opinion, that approach did fail him now and again. However, whatever Hoffman has done, unless I've missed something, has been consistently excellent, as has Day-Lewis, as has Philip Seymour Hoffman, as has Toni Collette. To solve a mystery, you do need a kind of hypothesis, or at least a suggestion.

Let's suggest a list of steps to character that leads to somewhere interesting.

1. Come to a total understanding of the character's mess.
2. Own the character's mess for an extended period of time so that you are no longer acting from sympathy for the

character, or empathy because you might have been in a similar predicament yourself.

3. Allow yourself to have an artistic vision and develop a unique physical formula of the character through Idiosyncratic Transformation.
4. Join 2 and 3, embedding the mess into the physical work.
5. Walk that in over an extended period of time till the mess and the physical formula have melded completely. At this point you should be existing and behaving as a completely unique entity, the character.
6. Understand where you are "feeling" that powerful sensation of character within your body.
7. Let that be the starting place each time you want to slip into character for the performance or shoot.

If the list above is achievable as your homework for character creation, the "place" is possibly going to be different for each character. Or perhaps not. Some actors use the same place each time to seat the sensation of character within themselves. Either way, from there comes a confidence that it is *there*, wherever that *there* is. There's no need to try to push anything or sell anything. It's just there and always will be. You can rely on it.

The Possible Someone

CHARACTER SENSATION and TEXT ANALYSIS

What is most important in that list is this notion of Character Sensation. It's an undeniable force when you're there. It can't be pretended. It can't be falsified. It can't be done by half. It can only happen when the homework of the mess has been done completely. It can only happen when the actor has found the inspiration to give him or herself to that character. It drives action, dictates behavior, propagates moments of astonishment and surprise, danger and unpredictability. It is the "feeling of acting" that is the result of all the other homework and the end result of the application of the technique to the subject. It is the "closh", the unique sound of the bell. It is the feeling of the sunflower at the end Van Gogh's brush strokes. And not any sunflower. That sunflower.

Let's imagine then, that the process outlined above can be utilized effectively by great actors naturally most of the time. I have had actors come to my studio and be able to do all of that stuff naturally. However I've never met one who can do it consistently. I watch them come in with texts that inspire them and work for them and do them well. Fine. Now here's Julius Caesar. And suddenly they hit a wall. What is that wall that we all tend to hit from time to time that stops us being able to access and play certain characters and penetrate certain texts? "I don't get this character". "I can't identify with this character". "I don't like this script". "I hate this writer". "No one talks like that. Can I change the words?" Such are some of the many resistant cries of the actor who doesn't immediately identify with a character or a text. Of course what they are really saying to me, their teacher, is,

147

"I don't have the wherewithal to understand this and play it truthfully, and no I'm not going to go looking for why this is a great role." And from that point, "I don't want to learn a technique that will make me capable of playing any character from any text. That's work. I want to change scripts till I find something easy for me and can show off how good I already am to all these bad actors in your class."

Well that's fine, but you can go and show off somewhere else. The truth about what's happening to you is that you have read a script with which you have not immediately identified. You have become self-conscious. This is a great writer, possibly Shakespeare or Shaw or Chekhov and yet you don't get it. Your ego kicks in as a protection mechanism and begins to lay blame anywhere but at your own feet. It's dated! It's badly written! It's badly translated! It's too melodramatic! The character is two-dimensional! Those accusations towards the writer and his or her work are your fears. I'm afraid I will not appear cool and modern if I play this role. I'm not intelligent enough to see how good this writing is. It's good writing that's been lost in translation. It's the translator's fault. And I don't know anything about the process of translation to expand on that. I'm afraid I will play it melodramatically and therefore falsely because I can't see the truth in it. I'm afraid I'm not smart enough to see the myriad of dimensionality in this character.

What can you do? Stop being afraid. How do you stop being afraid? Trust yourself. How can you trust yourself if you doubt your own ability? Learn a technique that will give you real confidence in yourself and your approach to any text.

You see, if we follow the framework outlined above in another way, we are asking ourselves to gain a cerebral understanding of something and then allow it to translate into physical sensations that affect our body and voice and sensations so that our whole mechanism is acting rather than just our head. We need to be physically free to follow those sensations that are the result of somebody else's predicament. Every physical and psycho-physical acting technique is after this goal. There are question marks over the necessity of feeling real emotions in such techniques as The Method, and those questions are valid. At the same time, there are question marks over the insistence that emotion in acting is irrelevant as some practitioners would suggest because the movement on the stage is going to be choreographed or blocked anyway, so what you're "feeling" emotionally while you go through that choreography is neither here nor there and makes no difference to the audience's experience of the play. The central response there being that emotion in life effects behavior and therefore if we credit the character with a natural, unique life we must then credit them with natural, unique feelings and ways of feeling that can then be used to formulate unique physical behavior, as such telling the story of the character in much deeper, specific and edgier ways.

But let's not get caught up in theoretical arguments too much. If we assume that you as an actor need to understand the text and you don't understand the text, what can you do? You can analyze it. Text analysis is not as scary or difficult as it is made out to be. It starts from the very simple Stanislavskian principles that he borrowed from Aristotle and made useful for himself and his actors. You have a set of circumstances given to you by the author of the play; that is where you are and who you are. What are those? Make a list. Try to be detailed and don't miss anything that may be helpful. When doing this, think of your senses. What does this place look like, sound like, smell like, taste like, feel like? What's the climate here? What's the era? If you don't know much about something that you discover, research it! It takes minutes on the internet to come to a basic understanding of Victorian London for example. You can do it and it's not that difficult. From getting a basic intellectual understanding of Victorian London you might find yourself feeling imaginative sensations about how it might feel to live under those conditions.

Ask yourself what your character wants and try to answer it in one sentence. "My character wants to marry Jane". Done. Now as we know, once we get into the deeper essence of the character, Multiple Objectives and internal contradictions, that singular Objective will become too simple to use, but it is always a good place to start.

Ask yourself what your character's Core Problem is and again articulate it in one simple sentence. "There is a plague on my country". More than likely your Objective will link up with what the character is doing to try to solve the Core Problem.

So now you have a basic cerebral or intellectual concept of what this script is about, what's happening in it and what your character is trying to do in it. It's at this point that actors begin to divert into individual ways of working, but all of those ways of working are concentrated on the idea of taking that understanding of the work and wondering how it will manifest on the stage or in front of the camera.

"What will this character look like, sound like and move like?" asks the idiosyncratic transformational actor who is now already on the road to creating a specific vision of a unique human being, working out the differences (separations) between him and the character, and beginning the process of bridging those differences in order to create a unique human life.

"How will I appear when I am in the costume and saying these words?" asks the actor who filters the character through himself, playing the character and at the same time offering a view of himself and his own personality to his audience.

In our work these two questions are set aside. They are not forgotten because they are important, but a better question is asked and that is "what is the best way of telling the story of this character and this play?" In other words, what is the right way to work? What are the best processes to engage? For who? For the audience.

Talking about your process as an actor can often sound self-serving and self-indulgent. I think that's why Daniel Day-Lewis and other fine actors refrain from doing so. "This is what I do to 'get into character'" has become a cringe-inducing statement because it implies some kind of immersion into a concentrated place that is a load of make-believe on the part of the actor and indeed all actors. That concentrated place does exist of course, but trying to explain it is like trying to make someone believe in ghosts without explaining the pathways to seeing ghosts. You can't do that because there are no pathways to seeing ghosts and there are no ghosts. But there are pathways to a total immersion in character (or as total as we want it to be). Without a thorough explanation of the logical pathways to reaching that place, it all sounds as fantastical as believing in ghosts and trying to convince everyone around you that you can see them when there's no logical pathway to seeing them. Therefore, within the dynamic of a TV talk show interview, there is nowhere near enough time to describe those pathways. To begin that description and not be able to finish it is much worse than just avoiding the question altogether.

So what are these logical pathways to an immersion in character that is *useful* in the telling of the story of the play or film to an audience? Everything that is not *useful* in the telling of the story to the audience is a load of make-believe that serves no one but the actor, and can in fact make that piece of work worse than it needs to be.

Let's then ask another question first. What will break the audience out of an immersive and interesting experience when they watch this piece of work? Certain forms of expressive theatre require the director and actors to create a cohesive physical and aesthetic poetry in which the audience may become submerged. Assuming that we are working within the genres of naturalism and realism for a moment, let's imagine then that the work needs to be naturally convincing. That means knowing the lines by rote, communicating with the character opposite, pursuing the character's Objective and playing the game like a child of believing without judgment in the fiction of the given circumstances. That's the basic stuff, easy and assumed at the advanced stages of the work.

However, when we are doing this successfully, something sometimes happens that breaks that convincing reality. We suddenly doubt ourselves and our homework. We become self-conscious. We worry about how the audience or the camera are perceiving the work. We literally worry about how we look. Am I ugly? Am I moving freely? Is this difficult to watch for the audience? Am I entertaining them? Are they bored? Am I 'feeling it'? Oh no I am not feeling anything! This means I'm acting badly! Am I giving a good performance? Why the hell am I thinking all this? I'm supposed to be 'in character'. I can't act! And so on goes the muddle-headed confusion of the self-conscious actor.

There's one answer and that's for me your teacher to say, cop on! Get over yourself and serve the character, the writing and the audience. You have a job to do so do it. That sometimes helps and sometimes doesn't and that differs from actor to actor. The better answer lies in a forensic examination of what is causing that to happen in the actor and to offer developed processes for getting into and staying involved in the right place.

Let's imagine that the cerebral understanding of the text needs to filter down into a physical ownership that fills the actor with useful sensations that can then be followed to create unique behavior for the character that eventually will occur subconsciously in the performance. If the head is full of all this guff and self-doubt, how can that cerebral understanding be there in the first place? It can't. The intellectual understanding of what is going on in the script is important yes, but after that any academic analysis is pointless unless that understanding is being used by the imagination to create a moving, physical performance. Sitting around and talking about the work is utterly pointless once the basic intellectual understanding is there. Now get on your feet and *move*. Play with the other actor. Allow yourself to be open to sensations that will probably translate into feelings that seem very real and, depending on the scene, high emotion in moments of loss or injustice that will arrest your entire system if you allow it to. Stop wondering if it's wrong. Let it happen. Then do it again and again and again making creative adjustments.

Let's briefly return to the stick exercise.

Are you seeing the dropping of the stick as a 'moment of learning' as opposed to a failure? It fell, but you think you know why. You lost your own balance. You pick it up, make an adjustment and try again. It falls again but this time you balanced it longer. And again, you think you know why. You make another adjustment and do it again. Soon, while working in this constructive manner you are balancing that stick calmly and peacefully right in front of your eyes like a snake charmer and his cobra. You've developed a *technique* for balancing the stick. That technique involves your balance, your breathing, your mental concentration, your feet, your hands, your eyes. You think about that technique and how it is developing *while working*, while applying it. Sitting around and talking about why the stick is wavering and falling gets you nowhere without applying the ideas. Doing it is everything. You will not become a better actor by intellectualizing your technique or the script. Yes, understand it intellectually. Read books like this one. But then do it, and each time is goes 'wrong' ask yourself why and try again with an adjustment in place. Doing the same thing again without making an adjustment of some effective kind is also pointless.

Then, once you are balancing the stick, try to think of anything other than balancing a stick. Think of your boyfriend, think of Jamaica, think of world peace and then, if you can, think of nothing. Once you have your technique down you should be able to act with only the character's thoughts going on. The character is not thinking about your acting technique. The character is thinking about the ghost he's just encountered, or Trigorin in the next room, or Angie in her bedroom. You should be in such command of your faculty once the homework has been done that you can cease to think about the act of acting and *be* the character by being completely wrapped up in *their* mess rather than your own.

After a while, though you have a sophisticated technique that involves many different aspects of you, you balance that stick without thinking about the technique at all. The technique becomes embodied. It becomes a natural part of you. When you act, you apply the technique to the new text as if it's a different kind of stick that you're balancing for the first time. You make a few adjustments and away you go. Soon you are running that scene or that play without any conscious contemplation or questioning of your technique or your homework or of yourself as an actor. That is the *only* way to come to the audience or the camera. After you have your technique down and embodied, the work on a new script should occur quickly and without anxiety.

You put the stick on your finger and after a few seconds of adjusting and reminding yourself of the feeling of balancing it, you're there and it's happening. As such if you have a screen test tomorrow and just got the script today you should be able to read it once, apply your technique to it, learn the lines by rote and run it a few times all in the space of about an hour. Then you're ready to take it to the audition with the *feeling of acting* and character sensation going on within you.

If you are questioning your ability or your approach to acting you have not got a technique that is embodied and that you trust. You're dropping the stick because you think you are a bad stick balancer. You're not acting well because you think you are a bad actor. Whatever it is that is making you feel that way, you have to weed it out and burn it, or at least learn to control that parasite so that it isn't controlling you.

Now, going back to the first questions I asked, what is the point of all this for the audience? When an actor is immersed in stuff that is *to do* with the character as opposed to being filled with distractions like self-consciousness that are not *to do* with the character, the audience *sees no actor*. Again, it's not a trick we're trying to play on them. Your name is Juliet to them. It's not your name anymore. You are acting smoothly and effortlessly as Juliet. The language is flowing through you and doesn't sound at all alien to you or your audience. Your voice fills the theatre because your triangulation if perfectly formed and you don't have to think about it. Your mind is filled with images and memories that belong to Juliet. Your body is filled with desires and indescribable sensations that belong entirely to Juliet. You have rehearsed and done your homework so thoroughly that you don't have to manipulate those sensations or your behavior. It all makes sense. You don't have to ask yourself if you are "in the right place" as an actor while you are acting. All that just goes away as if being washed downstream by a flood of "character sensation". The audience is with you, enthralled, following your story, engaging with you, feeling sensations themselves, not because you are trying to manipulate them but because they can't help but flow along with you.

The theatre is alive with Julietness.

The Possible Someone

EMBODIMENT

Embodiment is the process of transferring ideas into sensations. How is it possible that an idea or something purely cerebral can create sensations and feelings in the heart and body?

This is different for every actor, but most actors I train find that images are the most powerful tools to play with. An image can move you in extraordinary ways. Recently on Facebook a number of people have posted gruesome images with the dare attached: "No one can look at this for more than 15 seconds". Right there is a simple example of how an image can induce psychological and physical sensations that then cause behavior, turning away or turning it off. Let's be crude for a moment, pornography is the other obvious example, whether the reaction is arousal, amusement or disgust.

On a somewhat deeper level, however, artists can often come up with images that inspire the need to paint or write or compose. These can be concrete images from the life around them, or imagined pictures.

To allow something to affect you and give you the impetus to create art is a handy tool that can be developed. The best way to develop it is to change the way you look at the world around you. Try to imagine that everything has a humanity of sorts, even objects. Imagine that even a chair or table has as much *meaning* as a work of art. Endow simple objects with artistic, natural or human meaning. Take nothing for granted. Look at the ceiling above your head and the floor beneath your feet and consider those things as having been built by someone, fussed over, perfected and finished. Or if they have not been perfected or finished try to see them as perhaps meaningfully incomplete.

A wonderful actor I recently trained was playing a character that had been sentenced to a prison term. He was locked up in this horrid place, surrounded by animals. When we broached Character Memory and Imagery work, he was visited by a constant image of the car park of the prison. It seemed odd. Surely he needed to be building the images of the internal life of the prison, or perhaps the court room and Judge that sentenced him, or perhaps the moment of committing the crime. However this image of the car park wouldn't leave him alone. There was something lonely and devoid about it. The outside world pulling up and driving away, which he could do no more. Something indescribable. And that's the thing. You don't need to be able to describe it. What's important is that it affects you. It brings you into a useful place that is not just an intellectual concept, not just an academic idea, but something that moves you, inspires you and gives rise to physical sensations that inform your character and lend to behavior.

Anything that doesn't filter down into the system of your body and sensations is little more than a good idea. In my training of actors I have been able to loosely categorize them into three groups; those who have good ideas and are able to allow them to affect them and the work, those with good ideas who can't utilize them because they cannot allow then to be effective, and those who just don't have good ideas and need to be fed inspirational ideas by a director or teacher. I enjoy training all of them, but in the second and third instances I cannot settle for feeding ideas to the student actor because at some point they are going to have to separate from me and go out into the world. My job is to teach them to open up their imaginative capacities and allow the inspirational stimuli around them in, and then use it.

Something out there must *affect* you. What is it? The crying of a baby? A sad movie? The laughter of children in a playground? What strikes you deep in that human part of you? What affects you?

Once you can pinpoint one thing that affects you, you can then take things that don't and ask yourself to see the humanity, the joy or the tragedy in that thing's existence. It's a process of sensitization as powerful as Strasberg's work and yet much broader than your own experience. You can invent seemingly odd stimuli, like the car park, and as long as it works for you, no one need know about it and no one has the right to poo-poo your process. I might question you on it, but don't worry if you can't answer it. I know what's going on. I know what process has been opened up in you. I might suggest you try something else. It might work or it might not. It might simply be another thing that might work for me as an actor, but this is not about me as an actor, it's about you. So at this level your teacher should be giving you the space to be a little ambiguous. It's an individual way of penetrating the artistry within you. The individual artist in you is being formed. It's a very important time in your development.

The Possible Someone

MULTIPLE OBJECTIVES DIAGRAM (A PICTURE OF THE MESS)

As you are creating the individual life of your character, formulating their unique mess, it is often helpful to draw a diagram or a picture of it. Sometimes it can look a little crazy and indeed it should be something that one would have to explain to someone else. The way we do this in class is fairly simple in that we draw a picture of a human figure, even if it's just a stick figure. From that figure the actor draws arrows leading this way and that and names them as the various Objectives and passions that are pulling the character in various different directions. As such you can get a very palpable picture of the internal struggle and contradictions of the character. An area of the body is circled that is the place where the actor feels that character sensation when playing the role.

If you don't find it too personal, you can do this with yourself. Ask yourself what is going on in you. What makes up you? What directions are you being pulled in? You will have arrows going everywhere. One might be going in one way towards the desire for excellence in your acting, and another going another way that might be your fear that you are not good enough. You will have sex drive going one way and your apathy going another. Your will to change the world for the better, will oppose your sense of futility. Your confidences and fears will be pulling and opposing each other and that figure in the middle will be the epitome of the wonderful crisis that is you.

It's fun to do and serves one main purpose and that's to give you the opportunity to stand back from it and take a look.

You see, when you develop all this complexity in your character, it's all going on within you. You can make notes about it, sure, but it's very difficult to actually *see* it as such. It can feel like a lot of invisible forces working inside your body and system and that which is invisible often leads us to doubt if it all really exists at all. We ask ourselves, "am I just kidding myself?" "Is this all an act of self-delusion that the audience is never going to see happening anyway?" So you draw it on a white board or on a big flipchart, take a step back and see just what you have created as if it is almost a complex, scientific diagram. Then you know it's real. It's everything you have discovered about the complex, messed up human being you have been working on.

Sometimes you need to pinpoint what stage of the play the character is in when they are in the mess of that diagram. For example, Nina in Act One of The Seagull is a mess already, but her mess in the final scene is of a whole other magnitude. Macbeth in Act 1 is a distant memory when you think about the Macbeth of Act 5. You might want to draw a couple of diagrams and step back, take a look and see how the character has changed.

WORDS ON A RIVER OF SENSATIONS

Now entertain conjecture of this.

Imagine that the words of the script, that is your character's words, are a leaf floating on an ocean.

Don't worry. Dave hasn't floated into ethereal land. It is a metaphor that helps to explain a very important point for my students that surfaces at various moments in the learning process, but usually towards the end. Much of the time even very good professional actors fall into the trap of reading the lines and, albeit subconsciously, asking themselves what they are going to *do* with the line. How am I going to deliver that? How am I going to emphasize that phrase? Classical texts seem to bother us the most. I don't talk like that, so how will I say that line?

Let's look at Shakespeare for a moment. Now that I've had you imagine a leaf on an ocean, imagine that a man called Shakespeare is sitting down with his quill and writing in what seems like a kind of dream state, or a state of ecstasy. He has these incredible, complex thoughts that he wants to convey using images and metaphor and antithesis, and he is channeling those immense thoughts through his talent as a writer as the words come out onto the page. It is the thoughts that count. The words are a product of the thoughts. They are like a leaf being tossed around on an ocean, lightly flipping here and there, being pushed and occasionally swamped. Sometimes the thoughts are driving the leaf along, sometimes they are flowing beneath the leaf and the leaf seems to be staying still. The ocean is the thing. The leaf is something that fell on it accidentally or at least incidentally.

This may actually be the way in which Shakespeare might have written his works. There is some evidence that his first drafts barely needed correction much of the time. And if you think about the immense body of work he produced, he couldn't have sat around for years as writers these days are expected to do, ruminating over the text in the hope that some funding body will give you some money to produce it. In Shakespeare's time you wrote and performed, quickly, strongly and cheaply. In order to write like this in the right way, a writer needs to be writing on a sea of inspiration that is creating thoughts that are flowing into expressive words on a page.

Acting is not much different, and as we know Shakespeare was an actor also and by all accounts a very fine one. If the words are the leaf, then for the actor the ocean is the immense sea of sensations that is driving the character through the play. Sometimes those sensations are tempest tossed, sometimes they are calm, at other times they are seething and brooding, and the leaf, sitting atop that mess of sensations, is moving accordingly.

Prepare. Get the mess, the essence of the character, the sea of sensations working within your body and let the words out. The difference here between the actor and the writer is that the writer is transferring inspired thoughts into words. In the actor words are being tossed around on a sea of sensations and, as in life, the thought often comes after the word, like a breeze perhaps, moving in to play with the leaf also, but only afterwards.

Take any line of Shakespeare and try it for yourself. "I have of late and wherefore I know not lost all my mirth." Place your homework, the mess and essence of your Hamlet within you, look up at Rosencrantz and Guildenstern (who you have just discovered have been sent by the King and Queen to essentially spy on you) and let the line forth. Don't try to *do anything* with the line. The words will take care of themselves, just like the leaf on the ocean. The ocean doesn't have to worry about the leaf. In fact it doesn't even know it's there. Then let the thought come after the line like a breeze.

Sensations – words - thought.

Ocean – leaf – breeze.

I don't trust you, but I'll give you something (Not cerebral but felt in the body) – I have of late and wherefore I know not lost all my mirth – My goodness, I am sad and I just got sadder because my friends are spies.

Now it doesn't have to be that, but it might go something like that, and of course I'm only wording it so logically here to illustrate a point. You don't need to be able to explain every line you say like that, although you probably could if you were asked. Of course your vocal training, which is now innate because you practice it *every day* is supporting you, wrapping around the words without you having to manipulate it, drawing the wonderful sounds and alliteration out of Shakespeare's poetic speaking, naturally emphasizing masculine and feminine beats and driving to the final word of the phrase.

I've used Shakespeare as an example here, but this model, I believe, is true of all text. The moment you feel yourself trying to *do something* with the words, your attention falls off the sensations moving through your body and system. It is of little wonder that Artaud and Decroux were so frustrated by the entrenched, word-based, scripted theatre of Racine and his contemporaries. And it wasn't, I think, a problem with the words, but the way the words were being used by actors and directors. You see, if Shakespeare wrote with inspiration as I'm suggesting here, the last thing he wanted you as an actor to do is to sit down and pore over his work, trying to "solve" it in some way and work out "how to say it" as if it's not even English anymore but some kind of alien language. He doesn't want your reverence. He wants your body, mind and spirit to be driven by the character in the text and for the words to be a kind of electrical charge, a result, created by a storm of sensations. Without the character and his sensations, the words are nothing.

Theatre and film are visual media and always have been. Yet so many actors freeze up at the idea of the words. Acting becomes about learning the words, saying the words believably, making the words sound right and fussing over the written text. But quite simply, that's not the process of acting. Any writer worth their salt has already found the right words for you and the character through an artistic process called writing. You must transcend the words. Your job now is not to somehow solve the writer's words as if the words are some sort of puzzle that the writer has presented you with, but to dig into the essence of the character, to find their mess, their body and their behavior and to let the words be purely an audio effect of all that other work.

ENDOWMENT OF THE OTHER

Endowment is a word that is bandied around in drama and drama schools a lot. It generally means endowing an object with a certain quality to help to make it meaningful to you and your audience. For example you may have a fake, plastic dagger, but if you endow it with the weight and feeling of a real, metal dagger the audience will accept it as such and so will you.

Another usage of endowment that works particularly well for my students, and indeed for me as an actor, is the work of endowing the other actor in the scene with the quality of the character rather than the actor. Sounds simple enough and it is, but when you really concentrate on it, it can do all manner of incredible things to your performance, none more valuable than once again concentrating you into a direct and extraordinary focus on your character rather than yourself. You see your character is defined partly by its relationship to the other characters in the play. How your character deals with other people also makes up the *kind of person* your character is. To some extent it is defined by its relationships. These are very individual reactions to others as ours are in life. Let's look into this a bit now.

Try it out. Sit opposite another actor who is nothing more or less than your colleague in the studio. Look at them, smile, have a non-verbal communication for a minute or so. You will notice that the person opposite you has a certain essence that is them. He looks like him, smells like him, sounds like him, *feels* like him. There is a certain feeling that he gives you and it's somewhere on that spectrum of love and hate. It's probably somewhere in the middle. Now swap partners and do the same thing. Notice that this new person opposite you makes you feel a certain way also and it is *different* to the way the previous person made you feel. It's not as simplistic as love or hate or something in between anymore. You notice that the essence or personality or soul, or whatever you want to call it, of that person opposite you is unique. They affect you like no one else can or does. What you are experiencing is the unique essence of the person sitting opposite you, uniquely felt by you and you alone. Your two essences are having a meeting. How they get on is the unique relationship that you have to that other person. No one else will relate to them quite the way you do.

Now close your eyes and put aside that unique essence you noticed opposite you and instead endow it with a character that is not the other actor in your studio. For example, imagine that person opposite you is your brother or sister. Take a moment to understand that and then to let it really filter into your system. Once you *know* that when you look up you will be looking at your brother or sister, open your eyes and look at the person opposite you. Suddenly you feel a sensation of the nature of a sibling coming from them. Try it again and imagine they are your lover. Close your eyes and put all that in place, how that feels and how it works within you. Open your eyes and look at them. It takes very little imaginative muscle to endow the other actor with the nature of the character in the scene. The actor is not your sister. It is the character's sister. It's not your lover, but the character's. However you can endow them with those qualities to the extent that you feel very real sensations of tenderness or affection towards them. In the case of the lover, you can actually make yourself feel quite horny if you choose to go that far. The point is the sensation you feel is not an intellectual idea or even an emotional sensation alone. It can be and indeed should be physical... within reason of course. Remember, you only need do what's necessary to tell the story.

Then close your eyes again and recall the sensation of your colleague in the acting class sitting opposite you. Put the lover or sibling idea aside and remember how you responded to them before. Now open your eyes again and look at the person opposite you. Yes, you have the ability to endow a person with certain qualities to the extent that you relate to them in a completely different way and then to revert right back to your original relationship within a matter of moments. It's a professional and useful way to work. It can be odd for anybody to relate to a fellow actor as a lover when you have a wife or husband and three kids at home whom you love. By endowing on this level you draw a definite line between the real world and the fiction, step into the fiction *in character* and step right out of it again at the end of the play or film or whatever it is. It gives both of you and the other actor complete permission to be in character and play the scene with absolute commitment, removing any awkwardness, which again is nothing more than an annoying distraction from telling the story.

Pile up the facts about the character. This person opposite me is my lover and husband, but he cheated on me and confessed and I have forgiven him, although it weighs on me. He is also the only person who can save a lot of people's lives in the town. Now when I, Elizabeth look up and start this scene I will be looking at John Proctor, not an actor and we will play this scene out from John and Elizabeth's perspective, looking out of their eyes, thinking their thoughts, feeling sensations that belong to them. If I behave a certain way I can be sure that it is not the manipulation of a distracted actor. It is the behavior of Elizabeth Proctor dealing with John and trying to solve a very tricky Core Problem. Together the actors live out the fiction by giving each other the permission to *be* fully committed to their roles. At the end of the rehearsal we take away the fiction, return to ourselves and have a chat with the director about how we got on.

The Possible Someone

USING THE COMMEDIA AS PHYSICAL PRACTICE

The toughest stuff in all of this work is doubtlessly the physical stuff. Idiosyncratic Transformation is a long process that can be wonderful and artistic but can also be frustrating. Let's look at why.

First of all, most actors who come to me are not whole. By that I mean their bodies are separated from their minds. They have developed a physical pattern over years of living pretty much in their heads and emotions and have not taken the time to consider their body as a living part of them. It's just a vehicle to get them around. Now there are some actors of course who are also dancers or have a history of physical theatre practice through forms like Corporeal Mime, Suzuki or Lecoq. These actors are already communicating with their bodies. In their acting their thoughts, sensations and bodies are reacting and responding together. However for most, especially those who are screen trained only, they are talking heads, like newsreaders behind desks. Their minds and bodies are not communicating. That of course needs to be solved if you want to have any hope of being able to utilize that body to create a physical character. You need to know it intimately so you can "talk" to it.

Secondly, the physical work is evident to the audience utterly. The internal work might exude to them or it might not. It's up for interpretation. They might think they have received some deeper layer of meaning and assume it is they who have interpreted that layer of meaning in the performance. They might not think it was you who had that working away within, and that it came out to them in exactly the way you planned it through your triangulation. How the work is received can remain slightly ambiguous. On one occasion when I was performing, there were three reviewers in the audience. One saw great layers of meaning in the work, which I had deliberately placed there. The second saw something in the performance they thought was excellent, but that I had not planned, and the third just didn't get any of it and thought it was all a load of crap. How an audience member reads the deeper layering of meaning in the work is not entirely in your control. You can only create it in the most artistic, diligent way you can and send it on out there for the world to either love or hate.

However, the physical stuff is right there. If that limp is unconvincing, you're in trouble. If that arc of the character's decent into illness and death is not properly built, the audience will see that in the most obvious ways because it is right there in front of their eyes. It's not up for interpretation. It either works or it doesn't. It's easy enough to make yourself feel feelings that seem real. Children do it all the time when they play. However making yourself feel physically that you are someone else moving through the world is a tougher job altogether. It takes time and patience and there will be stages of it that can feel truly awful before the work is properly embodied.

Harkening back to Daniel's Christy again, when I hear people call him self-indulgent or over-the-top for the work he did to get Christy physically right, it actually angers me. These are insults leveled by people who have no idea how tricky physical transformation can be. It is tough, often painful and exhausting, and it has to be intricately right. If you are going to go down that road to that place, you're going all the way. There are no half measures.

Many actors, including those I train, run a mile from this kind of work. For most it is simply too hard. And I can understand that. They start off with the best of intentions, but somewhere along the line tiredness or frustration kick in and they back out of it and concentrate on the internal work instead. They get to a point where they know they have to put something up in front of the class that isn't finished and it doesn't work and feels disembodied and embarrassing. I know because I've been there myself. In fact in acting school I was told to get my scene up onto the floor in front of the group and said I wasn't ready and was chastised for it. So I put it up there and sure enough I was scolded for it. In fact the teacher asked me what the hell I thought I was trying to achieve, because to him physical transformation was not even worth considering anyway.

In my studio, however, the mid-point of the process is not seen as a disastrous balls-up because everyone knows it's a mid-point and maybe not even that. There's no need for embarrassment. To the contrary, any attempt at physical transformation is applauded because everyone knows how tough it is and that it would be so much easier to ignore it like many actors and teachers do, stick your fingers in your ears and go la la la la la. You see, once you *try it*, even if it feels hopelessly wrong, you get a sense that you did in fact *change*. Something was different. You were seeing the world through the lense of another body, even if it was a kind of deformed fetus at the time. Any attempt at it gives you clues that you can either use or throw out. Every attempt is valuable. No attempt at all means nothing can ever happen.

It's a little bit like developing an accent. I always tell my students to go for it and go for it early. Be embarrassed. Get it wrong. Get it wrong right in front of the rest of the class. Because as much as you got it wrong, there will be at least some sounds that were right. I, and the rest of the class, can make a list for you of which were right and which were wrong and over the course of the rehearsals or the classes, we build that accent to a point of rightness until not even a native speaker could tell you weren't a native. Or at least we try really hard! How can you start the process of "getting it right" if you don't start the process? Further to that, you then have to speak with that accent all the time, or as much as you possibly can in life so that it becomes second nature to you. It's the same with Idiosyncratic Transformation. You are altering the entire shape of your body, the way it moves through space and performs tasks. You can't just come to class and try to throw it on. You need to walk it in at home, up the mountains, in the shower, wherever and whenever you can.

The attempt is the thing and if you are in a school where this kind of artistry is frowned upon or laughed at, get the hell out of there. "It's too hard, just do your own accent" or "why are you doing that with you body? Just do it as you! As long as it sounds convincing" is an insult to you, your audience and acting itself. Could you imagine Day-Lewis playing Jerry Conlon or Christy in his middle-class English accent? What a total insult to those characters. Their voice is part of them. It speaks of their history and their sense of place. Who are we to decide it's not necessary? Accents are part of that which makes us who we are. So is our physical self. Not all of us are good mimics or impersonators and it's not about trying to be one. However you can make yourself better at it by listening to other accents, tuning in and trying it.

As such you can make yourself better at physical transformation by trying it, playing with it and mucking around with it. The first step is to be physically flexible and mercurial. The way you hold yourself is only one way. Think of your body as a vehicle for character. Keep it fit and flexible. Go to the gym, do Yoga or Pilates or Alexander technique. Take a Suzuki, Viewpoints or Corporeal Mime class. These all help your body to remain adaptable. From there try changing it into different forms and shapes. A wonderful pallet to use for this work is the archetypes of the Commedia Del Arte.

The Commedia is a form of improvised theatre that has been around for many hundreds of years. It began in Italy and was appropriated by the French where Moliere used it most famously to create his masterful comedies. The Archetypes of the Commedia are evident in every comedy you will ever see from some of the oldest written texts right up to The Simpsons. Modern examples do not always fit exactly into the physical description, but the psychological life is usually reflective of the traditional form. The archetypes changed and evolved in different areas across Europe over hundreds of years, so the interpretations of them vary from one teacher to the next. However most of them have certain physical and psychological components that are common and can be useful to us to help to train our bodies.

Harlequin, or Arlequino is the mischief-maker, acrobatic, compact and strong. He provokes arguments and causes chaos among the other characters. He is physically grounded and his power is in his hips and thighs. Eg. Bart from the Simpsons, Hawkeye from Mash.

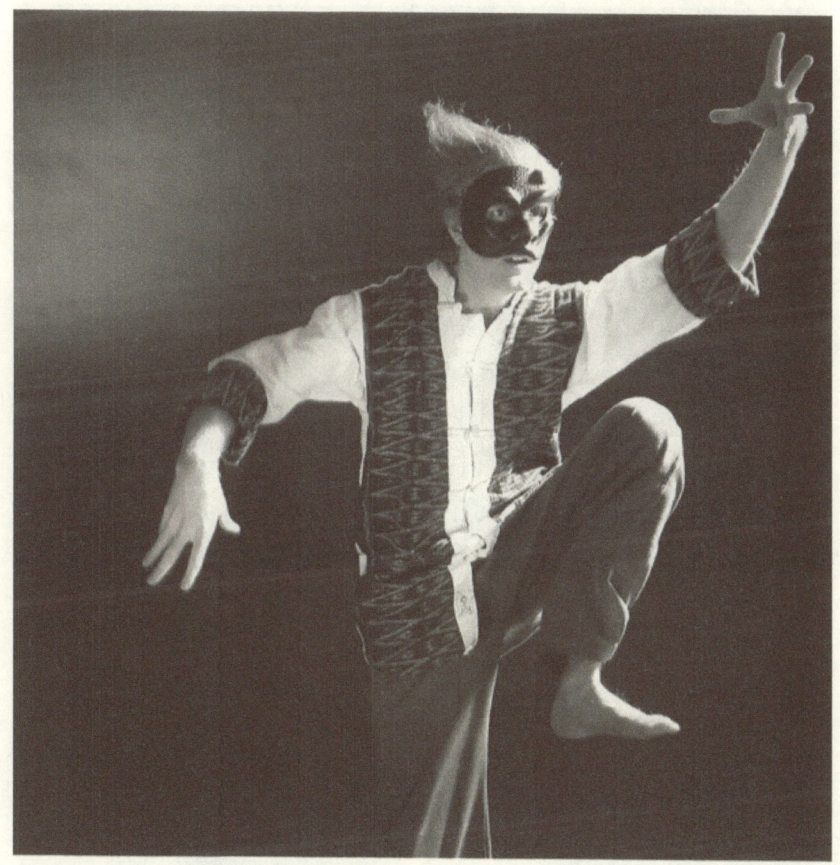

Pantalone is the old Jewish miser, spindly and money-obsessed. His nose, chin and long fingers lead him. Eg. Mr Burns from The Simpsons, Shylock.

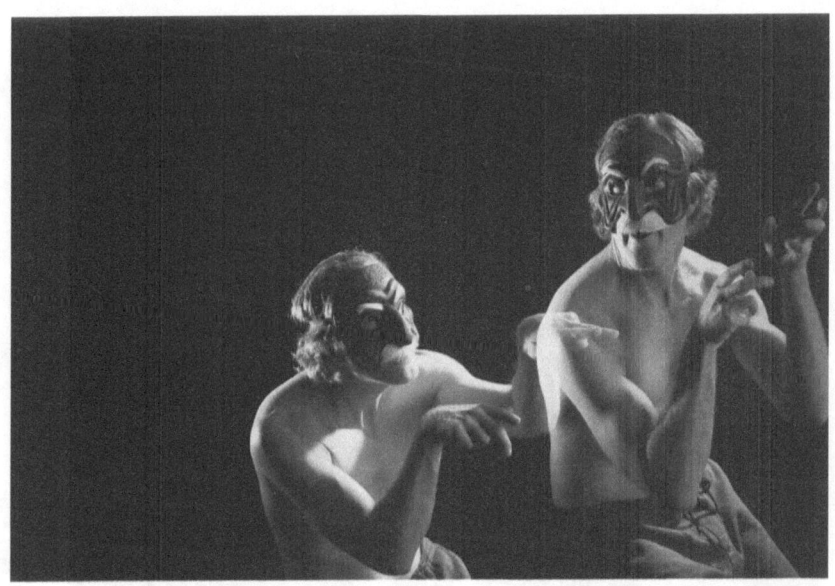

The Capitano is the chief of police or the head of the military, upright, a show-off and yet cowardly and dopey beneath. He leads from his chest. Eg. Don Quixote.

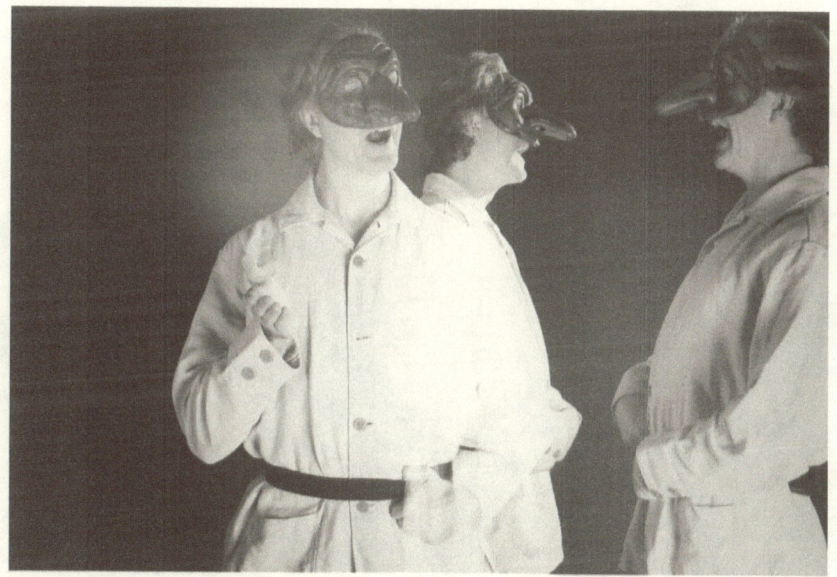

The Doctor is a quack. Quick and busy, he covers his lack of knowledge of medicine by going like the clappers about his business, treating all his patients with the same remedy, an enema. Eg. Doctor Nick Riviera from The Simpsons.

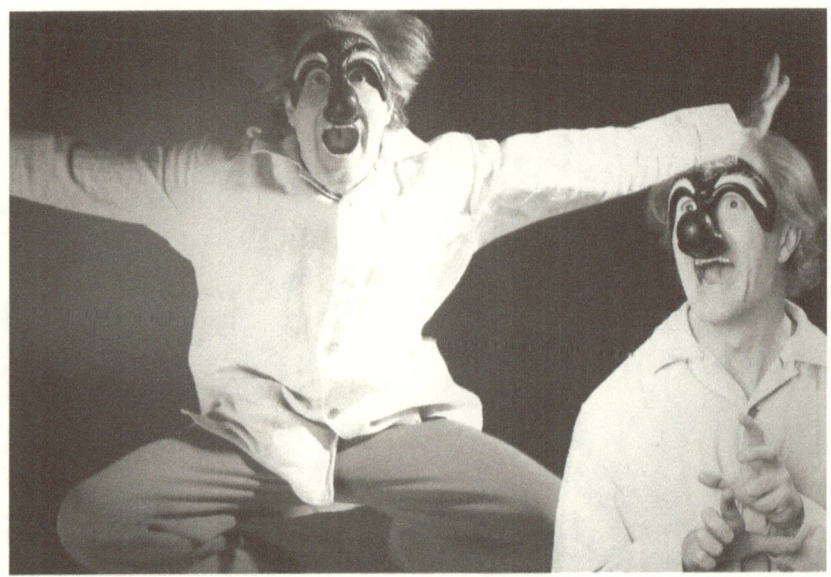

Brighella is a brute, weighty and fat. He is capable of great heroics and feats of romance if his laziness and obsessions with food and booze get out of the way. He leads with his belly. Eg. Homer from The Simpsons.

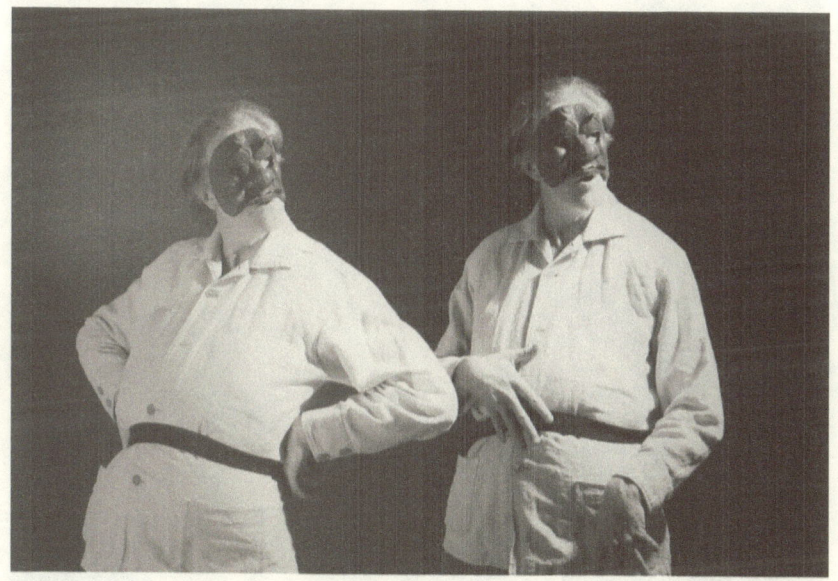

The Sad Clown is heart-broken. His body is drawn down, chest sunken, his hands covered by his too-long sleeves. He pines for a woman far out of his league. Eg. Milhouse from The Simpsons.

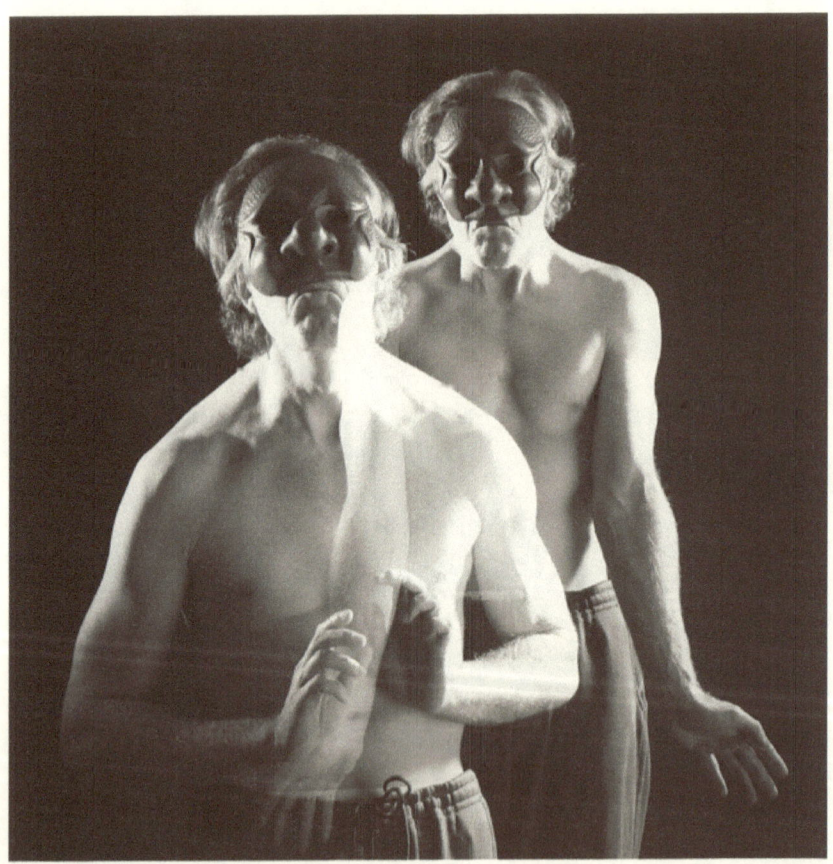

Just playing with these six archetypes is great exercise in training your body to take on the physical life of another character. They are uniquely physically shaped, very different from one another, and require a total change in your own physical patterns. If you can build them physically, commit to them totally, walk them in till they feel like second nature to you, make your breakfast as them and do your business as them, you will be able to alter your body in many other ways. As they are archetypes, more than likely most of the "realistic" characters you will play will not be as extreme, but what you will find is that most of your characters will fit into one or the other of them in some way, or you can use them as starting points for your work. Again I don't know, but Daniel Plainview seems to me to be a dark, dark version of Pantalone. Heath Ledger's Joker is a dark Harlequin. Don Quixote is a Capitano of almost perfect proportions. Constantine has many elements of the Sad Clown. You will also find yourself inventing your own "feeling" or version of each.

Remember these are not stereotypes or clichés. A stereotype is a cliché of a person that is meant to somehow inhabit or represent a community. For example, the limp-wristed, effeminate gay that's constantly after dirty sex from straight people. We all know it's a cliché that has been set up by people who don't particularly like gays and are actually afraid of them. There is no gay archetype. An archetype is a specific character from the Commedia that was designed not to insult a particular group or community but to be pitted against other characters in improvised performances in order to create crazy dramatic circumstances and comedic conflict. Harlequin is traditionally an escaped black slave, but he is not representative of all black people. His character dynamics are peculiar to him. Pantalone is traditionally Jewish, but again there is no suggestion that he represents all Jews. He has a name, an age, a physicality and an identity that are peculiar to him alone.

These are great ways to exercise your mind and body in the pursuit of a physical body that is open and adaptable to physical characterization. As with any skill or art, you need to practice it and hone it. It won't magically happen by itself. If you have a modicum of talent or a leaning towards this kind of acting, you need to start developing it as early as possible. Try researching these archetypes. Look at the old etchings and the masks and see if you can create for yourself an essential Harlequin, Pantalone, or indeed all of them.

There is nothing more wondrous and satisfying than a complete character sensation; that your mind, body, senses, voice and all are filled with the character's essence. Without the work on the body, it can never be quite complete, even though it may still work very well.

TRUST

"Faith and a Sense of Truth", Stanislavski emblazoned at the top of one of his chapters in An Actor Prepares. We know he was talking about belief in the circumstances and gaining a sense that what is happening is real. Let's look finally at the importance of trust in your work.

First of all there is no actor that has ever existed who has not, at some point or other, doubted herself and her work. There are huge pressures that come with being a professional actor. This is a piece of work that is going to be seen by people. People are judgmental. They will cast aspersions, make sweeping statements and judge from their own perspective what is good and what isn't.

What does an audience member mean when they say, "that was good?" They are saying, "that piece of work appealed to me". That's literally all it is. Why that particular piece of work appealed to them is to do only with them. It could be that they are elderly and there was an elderly character in the play. They liked that because they could relate to it. It could be that the play was a comedy and personally that's what they like to see in the theatre. Conversely, if they didn't like it, it means that for whatever reason they did not relate to it.

As artists, our choices are for us. We create works of art that have meaning, we think, for the wider society around us and for humanity as a whole. But there is no such thing as a total, single human reaction to the work. It may be popular because we have ensured that it appeals to a certain social dynamic, but that's a marketing choice, not an artistic one. As such, as long as we have made our choices for the right artistic reasons, not for personal aggrandizement or ego, we can confidently and courageously present our work to the world. As an actor, your thinking needs to be the same. You are making artistic choices and creating a work of art called a character for artistic reasons that you feel work and is important for people to see and consider. That's all there is too it.

In regards to reviews, statements will be made such as "the acting was good". Such a judgment that has little analysis attached to it and goes into little detail should be read as such. What is "good" acting? At the end of the day, good acting means that the story was told by the actors on the stage and no one in the audience felt that they were watching an actor struggling in some way through their performance, concerned about their choices and not trusting themselves enough to play the character, reveal the character's essence and tell their story. As such we should, at the advanced stages of the work, assume that the acting will be good. Whether someone feels it was good or not is not really our concern as long as we have made artistic and considered choices and placed our trust in them. Again it could be that the reviewer did not understand the genre or the style. There's no point being naturalistic in a melodrama, for example, and if someone doesn't like melodrama, they won't like the acting that's required for it.

In regards to training, look for that which is specific and structured, and of course forensic. If you're paying good money you deserve personalized attention. Yes, learning something new and complex can be difficult and you may hit walls, but the training should always be constructive. Any school or teacher that attacks you, insults you or demeans you usually has issues with its own ability or a distrust of its own systems. Anything that makes you feel less sure of yourself or leads you to a distrust of yourself as an actor is not good training. That said, you also need to know that you are there to be taught, not to be reassured. If your teacher tells you you're brilliant all day in order to keep you coming back to the school and paying more fees, that's bogus too. Don't take constructive criticism personally. Consider that it might be a golden key to your next step as an actor.

The big question that plagues all training actors as they watch the likes of Bryan Cranston or Philip Seymour Hoffman or Cate Blanchet is, "am I as good as them?" The answer is yes *if* you are doing what they are doing; or better said not doing what they are not doing. They are not winging it. They are not distrustful of their technique, their approach or their decisions. They are not wondering if they are smart enough, pretty enough or brave enough. They are not crossing their fingers and trying to get away with it. They are not concerned that someone will think they're pretentious because they build characters. They are working.

And I think its important to say that they do not allow reviews or criticism from any direction to affect that trust, or if they do then not for long. They are never totally satisfied with the work because they in a state of perpetual learning and development. However, they are concentrating on the work and the work is to take the subject of the character, interpret it, form it, work it in and put it on the stage or in front of the camera trusting that they have made interesting, artistic choices that will serve the character and the story.

Just because someone is working and their head is on the TV or the cinema screen consistently doesn't mean they are a better actor than you if you have trained and brought yourself to a level that you trust. They are your peers. They have just had a little more luck or lived in a different town or got noticed in a way that has not befallen you.

Yet.

Don't be afraid to be an artist. Don't be afraid to be bold. You deserve it as much as anyone else.

Trust thyself.

D.

The Possible Someone

The Possible Someone

The Possible Someone

www.ingramcontent.com/pod-product-compliance
Lightning Source LLC
Chambersburg PA
CBHW032009170526
45157CB00002B/615